WITHDRAWN

Kristin G. Congdon

Community Art in Action

Davis Publications, Inc., Worcester, Massachusetts

ART EDUCATION IN PRACTICE SERIES

Marilyn G. Stewart

Editor

Kristin G. Congdon

Community Art in Action

Follow an art teacher around for a day—and then stand amazed. At any given moment, the art teacher has a ready knowledge of materials available for making and responding to art; lesson plans with objectives for student learning; resources for extending art learning to other subjects; and the capabilities, interests, and needs of the students in the art room. Often working with a schedule that requires shifting several times a day from working with students in preschool to those in elementary, middle, and high school, the art teacher decides what to teach, how to teach it, whether students have learned it, and what to do next. The need for rapid decision making in the art room is relentless.

The demands continue after school as the art teacher engages in assessment of student learning, curriculum planning, organization of materials, and a wide range of activities within the school community. Although most teachers want to be aware of and to integrate into their teaching new findings and developments within their field, they are pressed to find the time for routine, extensive reading of the literature.

Art Education in Practice provides the art teacher, museum educator, student, scholar, and layperson involved in art education with an overview of significant topics in art education theory and practice. The series is designed to meet the needs of art educators who want to know the issues within, the rationales provided for, and the practical implications of accepting curricular proposals presented from a variety of scholarly and political perspectives.

The emphasis of the series is on informed practice. Each text focuses on a topic that has received considerable attention in art education literature and advocacy statements, but one that has not always been accompanied by clear, concise, and accessible recommendations for the classroom. As new issues arise, books will be added to the series. The goal of the series is to complement the professional libraries of practitioners in the field of art education and, in turn, enhance the art-related lives of their students.

Editor's Introduction

Several years ago at the Tennessee Arts Academy, where Kristin Congdon and I were both guest workshop leaders, I attended a session in which Kristin told about a project that she and her colleague Doug Blandy had put together while at Bowling Green State University. The workshop audience listened intently as Kristin showed slides from the exhibition "Boats, Bait, and Fishing Paraphernalia: A Local Folk Aesthetic," curated by Congdon and Blandy and held in the University School of Art Gallery. I was amazed and intrigued as I listened to her explanation of how members of the university and local community rallied around the topic of fishing and were involved in providing materials for the exhibition as well as in the various educational events scheduled around it. I began to think, in ways I had not imagined before, of what it might mean to teach art with an emphasis on community.

Since that time, I have continued to learn from Kristin Congdon how to reconsider and extend my way of thinking about community and art education. Congdon's view is that the notion of community can refer to people living within a particular location, to those who share personal or group identification, or to groups who share common purposes or sets of beliefs. In addition, she stresses that art and aesthetic choices are at the heart of such communities. The author's expanded views about art, aesthetic decision making, and community are at the core of this informative and important book.

In recent years, art educators have been asked to develop programs that connect art making and the study of art to ideas about the environment, local history and tradition, multiculturalism, global awareness, diversity, social activism, contemporary art, and, in general, to extend the boundaries of art to embrace art forms often overlooked. In grounding her approach in the notion of community, the site at which all of these issues and ideas converge, Congdon brings to light important connections between art and everyday life. She discusses how folklife and community practices are associated with the natural and built environment, different occupations, recreational activities, ethnic traditions, and other origins of folklife tradition. She emphasizes the ways in which folk and traditional artists have forged connections between art and contemporary community life. Most importantly, from the perspective of the series of which this book is a part, she shows how art programs can be transformed to highlight these connections.

Art educators interested in helping their students make significant art-life connections will encounter many examples of community-based projects to serve as models for enhancing their own art programs. They will find activities for involving students in their own local community traditions, ideas for expanding student awareness of traditions in communities around the globe, and thought-provoking questions for lively discussion in the classroom. To assist them in their efforts, educators will find a glossary of terms associated with folklife traditions and community art. In addition, many of the programs and strategies suggested in the text lend themselves to the kind of interdisciplinary curriculum planning that has received so much attention within the educational community.

As editor of the series, it is my hope that readers will take the concepts featured and the resources provided in this enlightening text and use them to create programs within their own classrooms and communities, thereby assisting others in developing a deeper understanding of the power and the significance of art and the role it plays in our individual and shared lives.

Marilyn G. Stewart

Publisher: Wyatt Wade
Managing Editor: David Coen
Manufacturing: Georgiana Rock
Design: Jeannet Leendertse

Library of Congress Catalog Card Number: 2003114917
ISBN: 0-87192-631-8
10 9 8 7 6 5 4 3 2 1
Printed in the United States of America

For David
Who has worked to build community for over 30 years

Contents

Introduction: Art in Everyday Life

When asked what they hope participants will come to understand as a result of years of engagement in art experiences, art educators have a number of responses. They say that students need to understand such things as that "art is a significant part of our humanity," that "people, around the world and over time, have always sought ways to express their ideas and beliefs through artistic practices," or that "art can be found all around us, including in our own communities, and should therefore be acknowledged and understood." But when these same art educators are questioned about what they include in their art programs to assist students in understanding these important ideas, many teachers talk about lessons focusing on our best-known artists, Western art history, and, sometimes, art from places far away. While most of us believe that artistic practice is essential to the human experience, we often fail to address the artistic practices engaged in by people within our own communities.

In this respect, there is what might be called a "disconnect" between our ultimate goals and the content of our art programs. This problem exists, in large part, because we teach what and how we were taught, and for a long time this has included a heavy emphasis on the so-called fine arts and a modernist approach to art history.

This book addresses the gap between what we want to accomplish and what we typically teach. Its focus is on the art and artistic practices that can be found close to home—within our local community. It also presents a fresh look at how art educators can think about the idea of community. As we expand our view of what we mean by community and focus on the various ways people engage in artistic practices, we find that our definition of art expands as well. This broader perspective acknowledges the work of folklorists who examine the everyday artistic expressions of people living in cultural groups. Folklorists recognize that many artistic expressions are grounded in community beliefs and values. By employing a folkloric approach to art curriculum, we can better address those ideas that we have routinely identified as central to the study of art.

Once we begin to seriously consider the idea of community and to note the various kinds of communities in which one shares membership, it becomes clear that all well-formed communities are grounded in identifiable beliefs and values. Participating community members often engage in artistic practices that allow them to celebrate and enhance their beliefs and values. The beliefs and values are never static but change over time. Sometimes change within communities can be jarring due to challenges members must face. Challenges may be due to environmental change, new ideas about gender roles, an expanded diverse membership, or any number of circumstances that can cause a community to develop a new, transformed identity. Beliefs and values may need to expand or shift to accommodate new ways of thinking. Sometimes art and artistic practices, both innovative and traditional, can assist community members in thinking through issues needed to sustain a viable and healthy community. The work of artists and others involved with the arts often generates individual and collective action.

The focus on community throughout this book is consistent with calls in the art education field to embrace diversity and multiculturalism, as well as to promote a more connected relationship between the production and study of art and the daily experiences of our students. The artistic practices of community members are presented for serious study and consideration, but they are also meant to serve as models for ways in which our students can employ artistic means to address social issues and concerns in their own communities.

Broadening Our Perspective of Art

For most of the twentieth century, artists were thought of as talented and unusual individuals who created in isolated studios apart from daily activities. Similarly, a visit to an art museum or gallery was an activity intended to draw you away from mundane, everyday routines. Individuals who are academically educated in the visual arts feel comfortable in a museum, but for many others a museum is a place for the elite. Formalism, the most prevalent art theory in the twentieth century, taught us to focus on the form of the artwork—the shapes, colors, and textures presented. We were taught to think of content issues as secondary, if at all. Art was made by people who were geniuses. Their works were known as masterpieces and only certain people, well trained in formalism, had the knowledge to understand them. The hope was that all students could gain from learning these elite ideas and being exposed to works created by extraordinary individuals.

However, today's broadened theoretical perspectives, artistic practices, and artworks are changing what we value and how we think about art. Increasingly, artists, critics, and art educators are concerning themselves with issues and artistic expressions that relate to community life. While many of these creative expressions have been going on for decades, or even centuries, today there is heightened energy and interest in art that takes place in, and is meaningful to, everyday people.

These artistic efforts may be celebratory and ritualistic, associated with holidays like Thanksgiving, Day of the Dead, Carnival, or Kwanzaa. They may center on community events, such as a folk festival, a Fourth of July barbecue, or an event focused on ethnic pride such as a Saint Patrick's Day parade. People who think of themselves as artists, as well as people who create but don't label themselves by that name, can all be actively involved in these kinds of community-based arts. By their nature, many of these creations and events are family oriented and therefore involve children, adults, and the elderly. These community art productions may address aspects of local experience including issues that are religious, political, social, environmental, and economic.

Community-based art is increasingly being created and recognized in the academic art world and in the field of art education. While art education theory has not yet fully addressed community-based art education practices, there has been a great deal of theory-building leading up to it. This scholarship focuses on artwork that is cultural-based, collaborative, traditional, and ritualistic.[1] In other words, we are increasingly paying attention to, and valuing, work that is based in family and community practices. Wayne and Marty Scott make clown shoes for

1.1 *Wayne and Marty Scott, clown shoe makers from Howey-in-the-Hills, Florida. Photo by Bud Lee.*

clowns all over the United States. Being clowns themselves and members of the circus community taught them about the look, function, and wearability of clown shoes. In a similar manner, when Steve Phillip Stravrakis makes a sponge boat like those used by his ancestors in the Greek community of Tarpon Springs, Florida, he is speaking for generations of sponge divers. Their history and identity live on through his model boats. And when Carrine Porter makes her quilts, she reflects on community-based values of the hard work of her sharecropping heritage as well as on the pleasure of making beauty in response to the need to keep warm. Increasingly, art educators are looking to artistic practices in everyday life as they plan their instruction.

1.2 *Steve Phillip Stravrakis, Greek sponge model boat maker, Tarpon Springs, Florida. Photo by Bud Lee.*

Academically Trained Artists Create Community-Based Art

Academically trained artists also have become interested in art that is grounded in community life, and, in some cases, have facilitated community-based art. For example, in 1988–89, Judy Baca, a Mexican-American muralist from Los Angeles, designed and painted *Guadalupe Mural* in the small rural town of Guadalupe, California. While she played a leadership role in the project, hundreds of the town's residents collaborated. Placed in a park where teenagers often tagged graffiti and drank beer, this series of panels told the history of a farming community and its dreams for the future. For Baca, public art should be community-based. She views it as an educational enterprise that allows for a dialogue about issues related to race, ethnicity, class, and gender.[2]

In the past, academically trained artists were often designated to create what was known as "public art." In keeping with formalist traditions, the way a work fit into the landscape in terms of line, shape, texture, size, color, and materials was of prime importance to the artist. In response to both the wishes and demands of local people, many artists soon saw that approach as shortsighted. Works became more community-based, like Baca's murals, when the content of the work and the way it was created and displayed became more about local, collaborative artistic practices, aesthetics, and community content. For Baca, her work is not just about her specific way of seeing a community; it is also a collaborative expression of a particular community in a particular place.

An increasing number of contemporary artists agree with Baca's focus, as they work to educate and activate a community by creating art that explores a local issue. The work may relate to the issues Baca has identified or it might be directed at more political or ecological questions. For example, Richard Bolten's 1992 installation *Subject: Male Violence,* contained written reports, research papers, film clips, and audiotapes on domestic violence. This academically trained artist included stools, lamps, and tables in the gallery so people could study the effects of violence in this community.[3] While many people questioned whether Bolten's installation should be called art, it directly and emotionally dealt with a community-based issue in an art space. Other artists whose work is more easily identifiable as art create art that intentionally encourages debate and dialogue. For instance, in 1988 Elizabeth Sisco, Louis Hock, and David Avalos created a silkscreen photomontage, called *Welcome to America's Finest Tourist Plantation,* to draw attention to the plight of illegal immigrants in the San Diego area. The montage, placed on the back of numerous buses, was so controversial that the image—its placement and its message—was hotly debated all over the city. Media coverage from the event was collected and turned into a gallery exhibition. Editorials, newscasts, interviews, and informal conversations became a recognized part of the artwork.[4]

Baca, Bolten, Sisco, Hock, and Avalos are not considered folk or traditional artists, yet they do draw their inspiration from historical events, traditional practices (both positive and negative), and everyday practices. The work of these academically trained artists is rooted in specific communities, and it addresses the concerns, heritage, and daily practices of ordinary people. While taking this connective and collaborative approach to artwork may seem relatively new, it has actually been going on for a long time. Even though art historians and other art experts have generally ignored discussions of these approaches, for centuries folklorists have studied artists whose creative expressions are community-based.

Understanding the Folkloric Approach

Folklorists are academically trained to study traditional communities ethnographically. They identify people in specific communities who are known for carrying on traditions that are deeply rooted in cultural practices. Documentation may take the form of audiotaping, videotaping, photographing, drawing pictures, and taking notes. Folklorists often critique and interpret the traditional practices by placing them in a historical context that even the tradition-bearers may not be aware of. They are interested in all kinds of creative cultural expression including folktales, jokes, folk religion, folk healing, oral history, and ritualistic practices, as well as material culture and traditional art such as architecture, handmade furniture, gardens, and shrines. From the folklorist's perspective, a folk artist is someone who practices an artistic expression that is part of that person's cultural tradition. For example, hippies in the 1960s wore tie-dye shirts, embroidered and patched blue jeans, and often adorned themselves with the symbol of a peace sign. Orthodox iconographers, or painters of saints, follow specific conventions in their creation of biblical scenes. While each iconographer may be identifiable by a particular style, the rules that artist must follow are rooted in practices hundreds of years old. Often a cultural group appreciates an art product and experiences its functions on the basis of a set of standards they have developed. These standards may differ from those of the academic community. These artists are frequently referred to as folk artists, and their traditional practices are featured in this book.

1.3 Carrine Porter, quilt maker, Bascom, Florida. Photo by Bud Lee.

How This Book Is Organized

The artists mentioned in this book are often not specifically categorized as folk artists or academically trained artists. We are increasingly recognizing that artists learn from myriad experiences, and that defining artistic categories is more limiting than it is productive. What is most important for art educators is that students be encouraged to use a diverse group of artists as subjects for learning. In this way, students will understand that inspiration for art can come from anywhere, not just the museum or art classroom, and that artists who are academically trained often use everyday experiences as inspiration for their own creative endeavors.

As art, art history, aesthetics, and art education become more interdisciplinary and inclusive, a folklorist's contextual approach becomes more relevant. So too does the folklorist's content, which focuses on the creative expressions of everyday people in everyday life. Because the goal of art education is to teach art to everyone, a folkloric approach to art easily fits the art educator's mission.

Although this book focuses on community-based art and community-based practices, some "popular" or "fine art" practices will also be addressed. While many people have tried to draw boundaries among fine art, folk art, and popular art, these restrictions will not be stressed here. This noncategorical approach is used in order to allow for a full and uninterrupted appreciation of a wide range of artistic practices that take place in our communities on a regular basis.

In addition to expanding our notion of art and getting rid of rigid categorical boundaries, we need to identify what we mean by community. While people interpret this term in many ways, three of the most common are addressed in chapter 2: community as a location or site, community as shared personal or group identification, and community as common purpose or set of beliefs. An awareness of these multiple definitions can help educators to define what community means no matter where they teach.

Every art educator lives in a community rich in local history, natural resources, and folklife. For example, Northwest Ohio happens to have an abundant fishing culture, replete with tall tales of the fish that got away, lore about the best place (and way) to catch a walleye, as well as specialized fly ties, wrapped rods, and fishing boats. Local fishers are full of aesthetic advice, critical expertise on how to dress for a fishing trip, what to pack in a cooler, and what kinds of lures will attract the biggest fish. Art educators have developed art curriculum around these local traditions and daily life experiences as a way to broaden what can be seen as aesthetic, while celebrating a sense of place and connections to the local culture and environment.[5]

Educational theorists tell teachers what they need in order to prepare students to become involved citizens and contributing community members. We ask our students to become individuals who can deal effectively with the many challenges facing our society today, as well as people who can recognize and build on the positive characteristics of a given community.[6] This book aims to assist art educators in schools, museums, and other community organizations who wish to impart a message of careful, considered artistic involvement in local day-to-day activities that relate to traditional activities and environmental spaces. Folklore methodology is employed as a relevant way of achieving this goal. By practicing a folkloric approach, we ask questions about our common belief systems. We come to an understanding of why and how we differ from our neighbors. We develop approaches to appreciating diverse ways of thinking, and we learn how to integrate new ideas and expressive practices into our lives. We learn to be critical about our identities and evaluate our own traditions based on new contexts and future goals.

While chapter 2 looks at defining community, chapter 3 explores the many ways that folklife helps form communities. Chapter 4 focuses on ways in which current art education theory relates to community-based art programming.

The second half of the book explores artistic expressions as they relate to specific communities. Chapter 5 focuses on the natural and built environment where communities share a common location or site. Chapters 6, 7, and 8 focus on the second definition of community: the sharing of a personal or group identification. As we will see, occupation and recreational activities bond groups of people together. They share similar kinds of activities, knowledge, and ways of exploring the world. In a similar manner, ethnic identity often functions to bind groups of people together because they have similar histories, migration patterns, religious practices, and celebratory activities.

Much of the artwork in this book is intended to be used and understood outside a museum or gallery frame of reference. This newfound interest in community-based art presents art educators with many new challenges and opportunities besides merely changing the place where one goes to study and appreciate art. It gives them the opportunity to discuss a community's problems and possible solutions, local rituals and their artistic expressions, and the ways in which our material culture both separates us and binds us to one another.

Notes

1   See Doug Blandy and Kristin G. Congdon, eds. *Art in a Democracy* (New York: Teachers College Press, 1987); F. Graeme Chalmers, "Art Education as Ethnology," *Studies in Art Education* 22 , no. 3 (1981): 6–14; Paul Duncum, "Clearing the Decks for Dominant Culture: Toward a Contemporary Art Education," *Studies in Art Education* 31, no. 9 (1997): 207–15; Elizabeth Garber, "Teaching Art in the Context of Culture: A Study on the Borderlands," *Studies in Art Education* 36, no. 4 (1995): 218–32; and June McFee and Rogena M. Degge, *Art, Culture, and Environment: A Catalyst for Teaching* (Dubuque, IA: Kendall/Hunt, 1980).

2   Erika Doss, *Spirit Poles and Flying Pigs: Public Art and Cultural Democracy in American Communities* (Washington: Smithsonian Institution Press, 1995), 157–96.

3   Gay Morris, "Richard Bolten at Capp Street Project," *Art in America* (October 1992): 158–59.

4   Lucy R. Lippard, "Moving Targets/Moving Out." In Arlene Raven, ed., *Art in the Public Interest* (Ann Arbor: UMI Research Press, 1989), 209–28.

5   Doug Blandy and Kristin G. Congdon, "Community-Based Aesthetics as an Exhibition Catalyst and a Foundation for Community Involvement," *Studies in Art Education* 29, no. 4 (1998): 6–14.

6   See James A. Banks, "Multicultural Education: Approaches, Developments and Dimensions." In *Cultural Diversity and the Schools*, edited by J. Lynch, C. Modgil, and S. Modgil. Vol. 1, *Education for Cultural Diversity* (London: The Falmer Press, 1992), 83–94; Henry Giroux, *Border Crossings: Cultural Workers and the Politics of Education* (New York: Routledge, 1992); and bell hooks, *Teaching to Transgress: Education and the Practice of Freedom* (New York: Routledge, 1994).

Chapter

2

What Is a Community?

In order to understand and appreciate community-based artwork, it is important to recognize how diverse and pervasive communities are. We all belong to
many communities; even people who think of themselves as "non-joiners"
inevitably do join others in many kinds of community configurations. The study
of community-based art necessitates becoming aware of multiple definitions of
what constitutes a community.

People build communities in various ways. Although community usually is associated with place, today's many efficient communications systems allow us to build community through the Internet, or by quick and regular trips to meetings or social gatherings. Sometimes communities are built through common belief systems. You may not even know all the members of a community group to which you belong. For the purposes of this book, we will discuss community as consistent with three main situations in which people share:

- a specific location or site
- a personal group or group identification
- a common purpose or set of beliefs

Before specifically discussing these three principles of community, two points need to be made concerning all communities. First, communities affect aesthetic choices; and second, communities both adhere to tradition and change at the same time. Both these characteristics are important for art teachers to emphasize with students as they learn about community-based art practices.

Communities Affect Aesthetic Choices

The three principles that define community will be explored in this chapter in an effort to understand further how artistic activities can build community and bind members together. For example, while we may not often think about it, those of us who share a neighborhood need to come together to make joint decisions about common land use and traffic issues. Aesthetic decisions about kinds of foliage, benches, walkways, and public art are continually being made about local parks. When we share an environment with someone else, we feel responsible for aesthetic decisions that are made. Imagine that you are Cuban and you walk into a Cuban café that fails to reflect a certain Latin look. You might feel personally disappointed. If you belonged to a Greek Orthodox church you would have certain expectations about how the service takes place and how the icons should be presented. Your ideas about aesthetic presentation might be intense. While this kind of identification reflects a shared belief system, there may be other kinds of belief systems that bind us and affect our aesthetic choices. We may gain aesthetic satisfaction from a well-planned political rally put on by a group we belong to, or an orchid show if we belong to a flower-growers association.

Tradition and Change in Communities

Healthy communities maintain a balance between tradition and change, and too much shifting in either direction can cause a community to become unstable. Therefore, art activities that come from a community-based perspective are generally most successful when they recognize a community's traditions while expanding on them or challenging the viewer to see or engage in them in a new and different manner.[1] A park-planning committee, for instance, may identify a need to put in a new kind of walkway or select new materials to edge a garden, but the choices will probably be more successful if they are considered within the framework of the history of the park, how the park is used, and how the newly selected materials will relate to the rest of the neighborhood. If change is too extensive, it may not please the residents who use the park.

However, the intensity of an experience may be explained by a participant's first exposure to an event. The first time a child hunts for colorful Easter eggs, for example, may be the most joyful and pleasant egg hunt because of the newness of the experience, even though the eggs may be more colorful or the hiding places more clever another year.

It is important to remember that, when working with community-based aesthetics, some community groups will want, and perhaps even demand, innovation more readily than other communities. And sometimes, as is often the case in conservative religious communities, aesthetic choices are best when they are faithfully recreated, or as much like they were in decades or even centuries past. Whether a community is like traditional Williamsburg, for example, where a traditional aesthetic is appreciated, or like San Francisco, where diverse ideas and innovation are successful, community-based art programming encourages all people to engage in creative experiences as they relate to the individual's experience of being human.[2]

Community as Shared Specific Location or Site

Community, for many, means that people care about a specific place, often the neighborhood, city, town, or region in which they live. In Dublin, Ohio, for example, where farmland has quickly been replaced by suburban neighborhoods, Malcolm Cochran created huge sculptural ears of corn, which he repeatedly placed in a grid. His *Field of Corn* reminds people of the historical significance of the land. In my own hometown of Winter Park, Florida, residents are intensely concerned about increased traffic from a nearby neighborhood that is being developed on the site of a former navy base. Solutions are being found to calm traffic by bricking streets, narrowing roadways, increasing bike paths, and planting more oak trees. While these actions are largely rooted in aesthetics, they also communicate to drivers that they are in a residential space, which in turn slows them down to enjoy the scenery as they carefully navigate the territory.

Discussion Point

Willa Cather describes how the Navajo relate to the land in her book *Death Comes for the Archbishop* (New York: Vintage Books, 1927), 232–33. Read the following description and answer the following questions about late-twentieth-century earthworks.

"When they left the rock or tree or sand dune that had sheltered them for the night, the Navajo was careful to obliterate every trace of their temporary occupation. He buried the embers of the fire and the remnants of food, unpiled any stones he had piled together, filled up the holes he had scooped in the sand. Since this was exactly Jacinto's procedure, Father Latour judged that, just as it was the white man's way to assert himself in any landscape, then change it, make it over a little (at least to leave some mark of memorial of his sojourn), it was the Indian's way to pass through a country without disturbing anything: to pass and leave no trace, like fish through the water, or birds through the air."

Can artists create earthworks in this Navajo-like manner? What would they look like, or would you even be able to tell that an artwork had been created by human hands? What twentieth-century earthwork artists come closest to respecting the landscape in the way Cather described the Navajo did? Explain your answer.

Discussion Point

Residents from Tidewater, North Carolina, claim that "a best quilt is made from bought material rather than scraps and is used for guest beds." Ask someone who quilts in your community if he or she agrees. Explain the answer.

—Quote is from John Forrest's book, *Lord I'm Coming Home: Everyday Aesthetics in Tidewater North Carolina* (Ithaca: Cornell University Press, 1988), 76.

Discussion Point

In Gwylène Gallimard's project *Charleston/Atlanta/Alaska Challenge,* a stuffed teddy bear is placed on the exterior wall of the Historic Old Charleston City Jail, apart from other sections of the installation. This bear and its placement represent the far north's prohibition of children sleeping with teddy bears. Explain why anyone would insist on such a rule? Can you think of other kinds of rules like this one that exist in one part of the country or world and not another?

Caring about a specific place means that you participate in its well-being. A citizen of Twin Bridges, Montana, once told Charles Kuralt that "one of the first signs of the dissolution of a community is when they form a volunteer fire department. Hell, if there's a fire, *everybody* ought to be fighting it."[3] By this he means that it is everyone's responsibility to work toward saving a regional space, and in a rural area where fire is a real threat, select people should not be the only ones concerned and involved.

While most of us can understand this perspective and how it would relate to Twin Bridges, Montana, we might not be able to apply it to our own community. Most of us have no experience fighting fires, and are advised to call 911 and get the experts to do the job. This doesn't mean that we care any less about our community. In fact, different groups of people perceive their relationship with their environment in different ways. While one person stranded in the wilderness might know how to live off the land, someone else might not. The same is true for those of us who know how to easily negotiate our way through a major city, even if we can't speak the language and haven't been there before. We learn how to "read" our spaces based on our experiences and cultural understandings. Aesthetics play an important role in how we respond.[4]

Artists can help us understand our relationship to our varied and connected environmental experiences. Sometimes we are so involved in what goes on locally that we are not aware of how we are all connected in what we do, how we think about things, and how the borders between communities and group identities sometimes connect us and other times separate us. When we examine these similarities and differences, we are able to make better choices about how we live and how our aesthetic choices can have consequences.

In the summer of 2000, artist Gwylène Gallimard installed a major collaborative artwork in the courtyard and interior of the Old City Jail in Charleston, South Carolina. The project was titled *Charleston/Atlanta/Alaska Challenge: An Art Program: Contemporary, Environmental, Participatory*. As part of Charleston's Spoleto Arts Festival, it was hailed as one of the highlights of the summer. In order to prepare for the exhibition, Gallimard traveled more than two thousand miles down the Yukon in Alaska. She documented her interactions with people and her interactions with the environment. The journey continued through Atlanta and ended in South Carolina's Lowcountry, where the artist lives. The installation is about connecting people and ideas. In particular, it presented Native American ideas on the connection of art to life, which are often more visible and consciously synthesized than they are for individuals of European descent. Frank Martin, journalist for the *Charleston Post and Courier*, described what he saw:

2.1 and 2.2 Images of Gwylène Gallimard's installation Charleston/Atlanta/Alaska Challenge: An Art Program: Contemporary, Environmental, Participatory. *Spoleto, Charleston, South Carolina, 2000. Photos by Kristin G. Congdon.*

Try This

Write down a dream that you have for your community. Create a visual representation of that dream and place it in a bag (a dreambag). Exchange your bag with someone else and see if your partner can interpret your dream based on what you have created. When you are finished, read the written explanation of the dream. How close was the visual interpretation to the written one?

Try This

Long Island University uses art as a way to help first-year students become part of the university community. As part of a semester-long orientation, students discuss up to six sculptures as a way of breaking the ice, getting to know each other, and stimulating discussion.

Identify a new group or association in your community. Discuss a few local sculptures with them. Did the process help the group bond in any way? How?

Roughly, the dream river begins in Alaska, flows from North to South and frequently branches and forks into various eddies and harbors. A paper Salmon Slough is filled with drawn fish from students of St. James Santee Elementary School. The river then flows past a "Dreamwam," filled with "dream bags" (containers holding individual dreams and hopes) and a bay crowded with sailboats. This flows into a sand river which transforms into side tributaries composed of the sidewalk, and then integrates into a river of cobalt blue bottles, fed by a waterfall composed of indigo-dyed kudzu, contributed by artist Arianne King-Comer. It then flows to the Burke Harbor, created by students of Burke High School, moving onward through a substrate region with nicely executed negative color etchings of fish on laminated paper. The river finally empties into the Lowcountry of the Edisto where a barrage of Dream Catchers stand outstretched with large openings through which nightmares may pass but in which pleasant dreams may be retained.[5]

This large-scale project involved numerous community groups. It was both inside and outside the jail building, and included slides and video, and many kinds of symbols that communicated human interaction with the natural environment. Participants and viewers engaged in an understanding of their own identities in relationship to their environmental spaces, cultural beliefs, and ways of knowing the world, while connecting to the life experiences of another community culture. Instead of seeing aesthetic choices as individual, isolated, and nonfunctioning, the focus became connective and the consequences of the underlying aesthetic value system became more visible.

Community as Personal or Group Identification

We make decisions based on our ethnic, occupational, recreational, gender, and generational identity, as well as our sexual orientation, abilities/disabilities, and political identities. Economic class is also important. Based on these considerations, community groups or cultures vary as to what they find pleasing. Women in Sri Lanka often sew new sarongs and blouses so that the manufacturing marks show, whereas seamstresses from other cultural groups may hide such markings and want designer or company names to show only in carefully selected places.[6] Decisions we make about our clothing are only one of the ways that we show how aesthetic decisions vary among community groups. While most people in the United States separate their vegetable gardens from their flower gardens,

Discussion Point

Read the following quote and answer the question posed at the end.

"Successful community-based art keeps unfolding in the mind in the ways it allows real voices to be heard and the dignity and dilemmas of real communities to be felt and real dialogues across race and class to develop. Community-based art will never replace museum art. But museum art cannot substitute for what community-based art can do."

Do you agree with this statement? Why or why not? Can community-based art exist in a museum? Can you find examples? Can you plan an art project that would be rooted in your community and that would be best viewed in a museum space?

—From Michael Brenson, "Healing in Time," in Mary Jane Jacob ed., *Culture in Action* (Seattle: Bay Press, 1995), 27.

Discussion Point

"Can artists work in communities that are not their own?"

—Question posed by Mary Jane Jacob in "Outside the Loop" in Mary Jane Jacob, ed., *Culture in Action* (Seattle: Bay Press, 1995), 58.

2.3 Northwest Coast Native American totem pole dedication ceremony in front of the Canadian Broadcasting Company building in Vancouver, British Columbia, 1982. Photo by David C. Congdon.

Discussion Point

Years ago, the Chinese used to disable women by binding their feet. Among the Chinese, this practice was universally legitimated by writers, poets, philosophers, and diplomats. Small feet on women, even if they could not walk, were seen as beautiful. How do you think this could have been possible? Why do you think this practice ended? How do you think the culture was able to change its position? Can you name some practices people in your community view as beautiful, useful, or functionally pleasing that you disagree with? Do you wish to oppose that practice? How would you go about changing people's value systems on this practice?

African-Americans in the Los Angeles area are increasingly growing tomatoes, turnips, mustard greens, potatoes, peas, and okra among their flowers and shrubbery. This method of gardening has historical roots, and it relates to traditions that are medicinal, aesthetic, and spiritual.[7] If, for example, a gardener knows that growing a certain herb may help a particular ailment, then that understanding adds to the aesthetic pleasure of nurturing the plant.

Sometimes several kinds of cultural identities can work together to formulate an aesthetic decision. For example, Ellen Matthews describes a situation when her family sponsored a Vietnam refugee family. One man in the family, who was employed as a construction worker, began painting a downspout on a house with brown paint. The next day, when he returned to finish the job, he used white paint. While Matthews expressed displeasure at the man's decision-making process, she also knew that, in his mind, paint is paint, and the main point of paint is to use it to keep the metal from rusting.[8] The reactions of both individuals have to do with their cultural roots. Color didn't matter to the refugee as much as protecting the downspout, whereas the visual representation to Matthews, coming from a culture where paint could easily be found and paid for, was of extreme importance.

While the Vietnamese man's functional viewpoint of the downspout may be related to his cultural experience, the traditional art and aesthetic preferences of Northwest Coast Native Americans is often related to myths. A mask's purpose is to explain its supernatural origin as it lays the foundation for a ritual. Likewise, a Chilkat blanket is important, in part, because weaving is a gift brought by Raven from the spirit world to the Tlingit and other humans. The blanket commemorates and celebrates historical events in a clan's history. The blanket's natural form is perceived in dance; it is intended to be seen as movement.[9]

The artwork we surround ourselves with helps us define and redefine our cultural identities. It is rooted in history, ancestry, and ritual. Throughout our lifetime we adhere to these cultural identities even as we reshape who we are.

Community as Common Purpose or Set of Beliefs

This principle of community clearly relates to the two categories already discussed. A shared purpose or set of beliefs is the foundation of how people inhabit their neighborhood just as it is the basis for formulating people's identities. However, it is listed as a separate principle of community because doing so helps us focus on the importance of religion, one's political identity, or a social organization. Community, therefore, may be built around a church, temple, or other religious organization, or it could form around a political set of beliefs or activist group like the Sierra Club. It could also be rooted in a more socially oriented group like the Girl Scouts or Boy Scouts. While these organizations are not seen as religious or political, they do have strong belief systems that all members share.

Every religion includes rituals, and ritualistic practices all have an aesthetic dimension. A recent exhibition in Florida displayed numerous traditional objects used in religious ritual. These included *pakèts kongo* (charms) from the Vodou religion, Orisha *herramietas* (tools) from the Santaría religion, Orthodox icons used in Eastern Orthodox churches, and *psyanky* (Ukrainian Easter eggs). There were also objects associated with festivals, often deeply rooted in an ethnic group's belief system. These included *quinceanera* dresses worn by Latin girls when they turn fifteen, *papel picado* (paper cutwork) used on

Discussion Point

Read the following quote:

"To be costumed is to speak in the voice of another."

What does it mean? Can you give an example of this?

—From Barbara A. Babcock, "Too Many Too Few: Ritual Modes of Signification," *Semiotica* 23, nos. 3/4 (1978): 297.

"Art's about life, and it can't really be anything else. There isn't anything else."

—Damien Hirst quoted in Jerry Saltz's article "More Life: The Work of Damien Hirst," *Art in America* (June 1995): 85.

2.4 Junkanoo costume, Miami, Florida, 2001. Photo by Bud Lee.

Mexican Day of the Dead *ofrendas* (altars), papier-mâché piñatas, Cuban *comparsa* (stage company or masquerade group) dresses, and costumes worn for Carnival and Junkanoo festivals. All these objects have meanings that can best be understood when considered within their cultural context. People who engage in using these objects at the appropriate time and place confirm certain belief systems and ways of understanding their worlds. As the ritual is reenacted, participants feel that a balancing or reordering of the world takes place.[10]

Political or activist groups also employ art that helps promote belief systems. These include signs used at rallies by Democrats, Republicans, and Green Party members and buttons with slogans. Colors and mascots help express a group identity and bring people together under common causes. Fund-raisers for charity organizations also engage in creating and displaying visual objects used for rallying individuals toward a specific goal. Our lives are filled with stickers, refrigerator magnets, hats, T-shirts, brochures, and mailings promoting all kinds of ideas and belief systems. Sometimes we are swayed by the promotions, and we become more active or energized because of these objects. Professional graphic designers make many of the logos, posters, brochures, and billboards, but everyday people also create them.

Communities are formed in various ways around diverse belief structures, identities, and spaces. Healthy communities are constantly changing and adapting to new ideas and ways of thinking. They also adhere to traditional aspects that have been rethought and recreated. Understanding folklore theory and being able to identify community folklore is important in appreciating and, in some cases, creating community-based art.

Notes

1 Communities differ on how much innovation they choose to accommodate. For example, Sue Bender, in her book *Plain and Simple: A Woman's Journey to the Amish* (San Francisco: Harper, 1989), explains that among the Amish ostentation has traditionally been thought of as sinful. Because buttons may be seen as ornamentation, garment attachments must be hidden. Therefore, hooks and eyes are used. In this community, invention and use of varied materials are limited. In contrast, Tomas Ybarra-Frausto in his chapter titled "Rasquachismo: A Chicano Sensibility" in Richard Griswold del Castillo, Teresa McKenna, and Yvonne Yarbro-Bejarano, eds. *Chicano Art: Resistance and Affirmation, 1965–1985* (Los Angeles: Wight Gallery, UCLA, 1991), 155–62, claims that Chicano aesthetics involve *rasquache*. In contrast to the Amish, *rasquache* values the elaborate over the restrained. It celebrates flamboyance, high intensity, filling all available space.

2 For more on the idea that artistic experience, or making something special, is a part of our humanness, see Ellen Dissanayake's books *What Is Art for?* (Seattle: University of Washington Press, 1988) and *Homo Aestheticus: Where Art Comes from and Why* (New York: The Free Press, 1992).

3 The quote is from page 29 of Charles Kuralt's book *Charles Kuralt's America* (New York: Anchor Books, 1996).

4 For more on how various groups of people differ in their relationship to the land, see Giovanna Di Chiro "Nature as Community: The Convergence of Environment and Social Justice," in W. Cronon, ed. *Uncommon Ground: Rethinking the Human Place in Nature* (New York: W. W. Norton, 1996), 298–320. Additionally, Laurie Anne Whitt and Jennifer Daryl Slack have suggested that we need to rethink our traditional anthropocentric understanding of community so that "communities can be understood as sites where the human and other than human are drawn together in multiple articulations . . ." See their article "Communities, Environments, and Cultural Studies," *Cultural Studies* 8, no. 1 (1994): 5–31.

5 Frank Martin's article is "Work Captures Artist's Experiences," *Charleston Post and Courier*, Friday, June 9, 2000, A-14.

6 Ellen Dissanayake, *Homo Aestheticus,* 137.

7 Beverly J. Robinson, "Vernacular Spaces and Folklife Studies within Los Angeles' African-American Community," in *Home and Yard: Black Folk Life Expressions in Los Angeles* (Los Angeles: California Afro-American Museum, 1987), 19–27.

8 Ellen Matthews, *Culture Clash* (Chicago: Intercultural Press, Inc., 1982), 40.

9 For more information on masks, see Claude Lévi-Strauss, *The Way of the Masks* (Seattle: University of Washington Press, 1982), 105. For a better understanding on the public display of Chilkat blankets, see Steve Siporin, *American Folk Masters: The National Heritage Fellows* (New York: Harry N. Abrams, 1992). The specific information here comes from page 105.

10 For more information on the exhibition, "Florida Folklife: Traditional Arts in Contemporary Communities," see the catalog of the same title edited by Stephen Stuempfle (Miami: Historical Museum of Southern Florida, 1998).

Folklife and Community Practices

Folklife is the cultural practice that holds many communities together. As we saw in chapter 2, community can be defined in various ways. When groups of people worship together, work on political campaigns, share office space, or become part of the same Girl Scout troop, they develop common goals and aspirations. A communal language or way of talking about things that other people don't readily understand is often formulated. Jokes, proverbs, belief systems, material culture, and stories develop in the group. These forms of expression, as they are performed or created in a cultural group, are called folklife. Often the words "folklife" and "folklore" are interchangeable, although folklore is often thought of as the study of folklife. People who are academically trained to study folklife or folklore are called folklorists.

We All Have Folklife

Folklorists believe that all cultural groups have folklife. These traditional expressions provide individuals and communities with ways to artistically communicate their means of viewing the world.[1] Some folklorists have studied children's traditional play to explore children's ways of understanding the world. For young children, folklore may include building snow sculptures, forts (from a variety of materials), paper airplanes, cootie-catchers (sometimes called fortune-tellers), sandcastles, or handmade paper dolls. It may also include jokes, counting-out rhymes ("One potato, two potato . . ."), hand-clapping games, or jump-rope rhymes. There are also superstitions ("Step on a crack . . .") and holiday customs, like waiting for Santa Claus or the dance of the dragons on Chinese New Year. Children, like adults, often center their everyday activities around these folkloric rituals.

Children get the most enjoyment from their own folklore because they participate most fully in it. Folklore, therefore, has its own aesthetic dimensions usually best understood within the folk group from which it comes. A Japanese artist who was raised doing origami would be more adept at understanding the complexity of a detailed origami figure than someone who is not an origami expert. An individual who was not raised in a culture that practiced origami might enjoy the created shapes and representational forms but would not know as much about the difficulty of certain folds or the story of origin as the expert would. The Japanese origami expert has more information to take to the appreciation process than the person who knows little about the art form. As we learn more about the origami piece, we are able to view it in more diverse and interconnected ways.

Learning Folklife

Folklife is learned informally from family, friends, neighbors, or coworkers just by sharing a way of life. Traditions are generally passed down through families and small groups, although today folklore has a wider reach due to technology such as copy machines and e-mail. While art teachers may live in different parts of a state, they may still share similar experiences of young students who spill paint or parents who object to some artwork they see as inappropriate. These teachers may share knowledge of ways to make a puppet from a sock. Because their lives are shaped by similar circumstances, they can readily communicate with each other about their day-to-day experiences. They might do this in face-to-face meetings such as at conferences and professional development seminars, or in the form of listservs or dedicated chatrooms. Art teachers therefore may be considered members of a community or folk group whose members have their own folklife traditions and means of communicating with one another.

The way people within folk groups communicate with each other often incorporates the use of folk

3.1 Yasuko Dawson demonstrating origami in the Folk Artists in the Schools Program, Jacksonville, Florida. Photo by Peggy Bulger. Courtesy of the Florida Folklife Program, Department of State.

speech.[2] In Yoruba aesthetics the word "coolness" denotes proper custom. It is a gentleness of character, indicating the correct way to represent oneself as a human being.[3] Folk speech, while often connected to race or ethnicity, can also be associated with other cultural identifications, such as economic class. At the turn of the twentieth century, many U.S. citizens saw that upper-class people had carpets. When a family was able to afford one, they might say, "We achieved a carpet."[4] Sometimes the folk speech used by one group may sound derogatory to another. Beverly Hungry Wolf reports that within Blackfoot culture it is proper to call a grandmother either an old woman or an old lady,[5] while most grandmothers in other cultures might not be pleased with those titles. In the 1980s, a teenager might say something was "bitchin'" to indicate that it was good. One folklorist explains the changing folk speech used by young teens: "What was *neat* in the 1950s became *cool* in the 1960s, *rad* in the 1980s, and *fly* in the 1990s."[6] An art teacher might know what DBAE stands for or recognize the term "visual culture movement," whereas these terms may be foreign to people outside the art education field.

Different groups of artists use different kinds of folk speech that refers to various tools they use or the processes they employ. A quilter, for example, may refer to a "rolling" process, indicating that a quilting frame had been used and the quilt had been turned over to provide new fabric on which to sew.[7] Cowboy artists from Hispanic traditions may talk about their tools using anglicized Spanish names. "Riatia" or "lariat" is a rope from *la riata*, "taps" are stirrup covers from *tapaderos*, and a "marcarty" is a horsehair rope from the word *mecate*. Even the word "buckaroo" is from *vaquero*, the Spanish word for cowboy.[8]

Try This

Start a discussion around the following questions:

Do you know any hand-clapping rhymes (or jump-rope or counting-out rhymes)? Would you perform them for us? Does anyone have any variations? Why would these be considered folklore? Explain. Identify other kinds of folklore that you share as a group. What kinds of folklore do you share in your family? Can anyone in your family be considered a folk artist? If so, explain why.

Try This

Ask students to list five folk groups they belong to on a piece of paper. How is each group similar and how is each different? Students should describe what kinds of material culture are related to each folk group. Explain that these groups may center around any activity that is learned informally. When this task has been completed, list them on the board. Discuss the diversity that exists in the classroom.

Try This

Ask your students if they can think of any folklore related to their school. You can prompt the flow of ideas by suggesting tales about difficult assignments, lost papers, or ways they study for a hard test. Write the stories down and illustrate them. Put them together in a handmade book and share it with administrators and parents.

Discussion Point

Read the following quote and discuss what it means in relation to your specific neighborhood:

"If there is a basic principle of environmentalism, it is that diversity is good. Beyond good, it is a bottom-line necessity for natural systems to survive."

—From Jerry Mander, *In the Absence of the Sacred* (San Francisco: Sierra Club Books, 1991), 97.

Understanding Folklife

Sometimes, folk speech can be funny or political. It can describe how someone feels about his or her situation. The following joke is a good example: An African-American politician in an elevator says to a fellow passenger: "I'm not poor. I'm po'. I'm po'. I'm working my way up to poor."[9] The politician is communicating about his identity and the relationship of his race to economics.

Understanding and using folk speech can help folklorists and other outside group members better understand the work of folk artists. It helps illustrate the aesthetic dimensions of the culture from which the work originates.

Folklorists recognize that folklife can be negative and harmful. For example, minstrel shows, gang-produced graffiti, and some rap songs are all examples of folklife that can contribute to violence, racism, and unhealthy community life. But much folklife is positive and the recognition and celebration of positive folklife can help communities thrive.[10] Sometimes, because folklife is so integral to our daily lives, we don't think about it very much.

The next section focuses on traditional expressions in folklife areas, many of which overlap.

Areas of Folklife Expression

Folklife in the Natural and Built Environment

Many of us identify ourselves by the places we live. People who have lived in the same area for a long time often alter their spaces, making the environment more and more their own. Gardens grow and expand, houses are remodeled, and public places adhere to tradition as they change with the times. Folklife in the natural and built environment is often rooted in generations of tradition.

In the Little Havana section of Miami, Cubans, especially older men, play dominoes in the park as they share cups of Cuban coffee and talk about politics. The sound of clicking ivory *fichas*, or domino tiles, plays like a musical performance.[11] In Los Angeles, African-Americans grow food between flowers in their gardens. While this practice is partly economic, it also has medicinal, spiritual, and aesthetic roots.[12] In the South, African-American yards can still be found that are "swept clean," having no grass or vegetation in certain areas. The aesthetic, in this case, is related to life in slave quarters. Because the houses were so small, the yard became an extension of the laundry and the kitchen. Since a fire had to be prepared for cooking and washing clothes, it made sense to create a safe space outdoors. The function, then, helped support the aesthetics.[13]

Some people, including those of Italian descent, create shrines or altars in their yards, while others who are handy with tools may construct specialized mailboxes or colorful whirligigs. While folklorists may debate the traditional nature of some environmental art, more out-of-the-ordinary gardens or sites are gaining the art world's attention. While some folklife

3.2 Cuban men playing dominoes, Little Havana section of Miami. Photo by Bud Lee.

Discussion Point

After reading the following quote, describe the artists the author is talking about. Where do they live and what do they make? What clues support your idea?

"Their paints, too, were manufactured by their own hands—gathered from earths and plants and carbons from charcoal or soot; their brushes were made from yucca fronds and chicken feathers tied together and from horsehair. In other words, nothing was store bought because everything that went into making a bulto must be prepared with the utmost reverence; and although they did not have the actual relics of the saints to mix with their paints like the Russian monks who produced the Byzantine icons, they labored with the natural elements, sun, air, and earth and prayed all the while as they worked together in silence—like their Spanish ancestors had done for nearly three hundred years on that strange land they felt was so far from God."

—From Ana Castillo, *So Far from God* (New York: W. W. Norton and Company, 1993), 101–2.

(Note: This selection refers to the making of carved and painted *santos*, or wood carvings of saints. It is rooted in central New Mexico, and the artist is Mexican American.)

Discussion Point

Read the following quote. Where do you think the author lives? Draw the writer's wishes. Compare your picture with other interpretations. Explain why you depicted it the way you did. What aspects of your drawing relate to your own life experiences and places that you have been? Describe them.

"I want indigo buntings singing their couplets when I wake in the morning. I want to read *Joseph and His Brothers* again. I want oak leaves and dogwood blossoms and fireflies. I want to know how the land lies up Coon Hollow. I want Asher to find out what happens to moth-ear mites in the winter. I want to show Liddy and Brian the big rocks down in the creek hollow. I want to know much more about grand-daddy-longlegs. I want to write a novel. I want to go swimming naked in the hot sun down by the river.

"This is why I have stopped sleeping inside. A house is too small, too confining. I want the whole world, and the stars too".

—From Sue Hubbell, *A Country Year: Living the Questions* (New York: Harper & Row, 1983), 195.

is continued within a group's traditional practices, individuals within the group sometimes draw upon a tradition to create their own personal expressions.

Perhaps the most famous example is the Watts Towers on the south side of Los Angeles, built over three decades by Italian immigrant Simon Rodia. The focal point of this marvelous artwork consists of three towers, one more than one hundred feet tall, created from cement-covered steel rods embedded with a mosaic of broken bottles, tiles, plates, and seashells. Other well-known environments include

3.3 Simon Rodia's Watts Towers (detail), Watts section of Los Angeles. Photo by Kristin G. Congdon.

Howard Finster's Paradise Garden in Summerville, Georgia, which was built with numerous recycled objects, trees, shrubs, and flowers in praise of the world God created. Samuel Perry Dinsmoor constructed his own Garden of Eden in Lucas, Kansas. It is filled with about 150 concrete figures and thirty concrete trees illustrating Old Testament stories. Perhaps one of the most delightful environments is that created by Vollis Simpson from Lucama, North Carolina. His yard is filled with huge whirligigs, constructed from old machine parts. Some of them are over forty feet high. Covered with reflectors, the scene at night is like a carnival with moving lights. While most of these large-scale environmental gardens are created by men, some are made by women. Using bottles she gathered from the local dump in Simi Valley, California, Tressa Prisbrey built several glass houses, mostly to store and exhibit her collections of pencils, dolls, and other memorabilia.[14]

While these artistic environments may seem extreme, everyone can relate to the architecture of their town. Many communities have folk architecture, which is made by people who don't have academic training in building buildings. The structures generally relate directly to the climate and available materials. The Navajo, for example, still build hogans, and the Seminoles continue to make chickees. Cracker-style houses are found throughout the South along with dogtrots (pioneer homes built with breezeways in the middle) and shotguns (long, narrow homes, predominantly occupied by African-Americans, of which it was said that a shot fired from the front door would exit the back door without hitting a wall).

Our natural and built environment has a lot to do with how we learn about our world and our place in it. It functions to help formulate our aesthetic preferences. A careful examination of our own community's natural and built environment can help us articulate how our own aesthetic preferences have developed. This kind of study can also reveal the kinds of folk traditions that are continued by generations of our neighbors.

Occupational Folklife

When we think about occupational aesthetics, the first thing that comes to mind is the professions in which training in art is essential. These might include architecture, landscape design, and the graphic arts. We might even come up with professions like gravestone cutting, tattoo art, and window dressing. Folklorists have documented many other kinds of occupational aesthetics that might not occur to us at all.

Cowboys from the Northwest United States, known as buckaroos, are identified by their fancy

3.4 *Everett Gibson, custom saddle maker, with one of his saddles. White City, Oregon. Courtesy of the Randall V. Mills Folklore Archive, University of Oregon.*

Discussion Point

Elijah Pierce, an African-American carver of bas-reliefs, primarily saw himself as a barber who carved when he didn't have a client. Late in his life he stated, "I didn't even know I was an artist 'til they told me." Does someone need to identify himself or herself as an artist in order to be one? Why or why not?

Try This

Think of something that frightens you and create a scarecrow to scare it away. Use old objects you find around your house and place the scarecrow in a space that is appropriate to the fear. Explain whether or not it helps you get rid of your fear. Think about the objects you have used and explain how they have been transformed or whether they maintain their original identity. How does the success of your scarecrow relate to the objects you used?

saddles, inlaid silver spurs, and fancy lead ropes for their horses. Buckaroos go to great lengths to collect diverse colors of horsehair, especially white, to make their twisted ropes. Oregon ranchers are so adept at welding that they can create chairs from horseshoes, metal gates from miscellaneous tools and iron parts, and beautifully designed branding irons.[15]

One woman from Astoria, Oregon, who cleans tuna for a living, talks about her sensory experiences as she handles and cleans the fish. Farmers often talk about their pleasure in seeing an organized crop or garden with straight rows. And homemakers often comment on the smell of newly dried laundry when hung out on a sunny day.

An occupation often requires that an individual respond in an artistic manner. A farmer could create a scarecrow; whalers carved scrimshaw, and loggers whittle chains from single logs. Orthodontists trained at the University of Washington learn to make sculpture to hone their bending and welding techniques. They often continue making sculpture from wire long after they leave the university, sharing their work with friends at conferences and through photos in the mail.[16]

Other examples include sailors who make decorative and utilitarian knots, Vietnam veterans who decorate leather jackets, and boaters who make model ships and specialty boats like skiffs for the Everglades or Biloxi schooners for the Mississippi. In an office environment, cubicles can be decorated by puzzles, paperweights, posters, and humorous art created by copy machines.

Every community has certain kinds of work that help to give it its identity. Work helps determine ways of seeing and talking about the world. Once one becomes aware of the aesthetic dimensions of the work involved in various occupational groups, one begins to discover a wide and diverse range of occupational folklife.

Recreational Folklife

Most people derive great pleasure from what they do recreationally. Children are usually involved in numerous recreational activities. All kinds of hobbies, sports, clubs, and activities have their own folklife. Group members have certain ways of talking to one another, and often the aesthetic dimensions of the recreational activity are viewed as central to enjoyment.

Today decoys continue to be made by hand even though manufactured decoys can easily be purchased. While they are still used by some hunters, they are collected by all kinds of people. Indians made the first decoys from wood and cork, later stretching bird skins over frames of molded tin and cast iron. Today they are generally created by carefully carving and painting each figure to depict a bird's typical posture.[17]

Needlework functions as recreational activity for women all over North America. Decorative sewing exists in a wide variety of techniques. It can result in embroidery, quilting, crocheting, knitting, lace making, and garment construction. In the past these skills were employed to make necessary items for the household. Most women who engage in needlework today do so for pleasure. It is an activity valued by women from all economic classes.

People who are involved in sports often personalize their equipment. Surfers paint their boards, bowlers personalize bowling balls, and expert fishers wrap specialized rods with brightly colored threads.

Children's recreational folklife also has aesthetic dimensions. Young children draw hopscotch diagrams with chalk on cement sidewalks and make doll clothes and friendship bracelets. Forts are made from tree limbs and rocks; sand sculptures are formed in the shapes of castles, mermaids, and fish, while snow sculptures vary in sophistication from simple snow forms to elaborate dragons or cars. In some parts of

Try This

Interview someone about his or her occupation. Ask what kinds of routine things this person does in his or her daily work that gives aesthetic pleasure. See if the interviewee can describe the pleasure. Share your information with the class. How many of the responses involve something you might call art?

Try This

List the recreational activities in which members of your family participate. Be sure to include hobbies as well as sports and games. Name all the material culture objects you can think of that are associated with these activities. Can any of these objects be considered folk art? Why or why not?

Try This

In Bend, Oregon, there is a folk-art environment called the Funny Farm. The people who live there have a garden made out of old bowling balls. They place them on metal sticks, which are rooted into the ground. Over time, the sunshine changes the color of the balls. People from all over retire their bowling bowls in the garden at the Funny Farm.

Make a plan for a garden made out of some other kind of sports equipment. Where would you put it and how might it be received in your community?

Discussion Point

Discuss the different kinds of hats, shirts, jackets, and other clothing people wear when they participate in recreational activities. Include patches, logos, and pins in your discussion. Describe when an adaptation to a specific recreational outfit is seen as pleasing and when it is not. Explain your answer. Do others agree with you?

the country snow sculptures are spray painted after being shaped. More commonly, snowmen are dressed with hats and vests.

Many people collect memorabilia as a pastime. Collections may be of Pez dispensers, refrigerator magnets, salt and pepper shakers, cake-decorating utensils, old game boards, or fishing lures. Many clubs such as automobile clubs and train-spotting groups have specialized hats and T-shirts.

Recreational folklife is fun to talk about in a classroom because it can be very original and humorous, while, at the same time, accessible to many different students.

Ethnic Folklife

Everyone has ethnic identity. Some people identify with their ethnic traditions more strongly than others. In our pluralistic society, adhering to ethnic identity can help give one a sense of place—of belonging and rootedness. It can also cause problems when people become so strongly focused on their ethnicity and the values and traditions that go with it that they don't have tolerance or acceptance for others.

Most of us belong to more than one ethnic group and have trouble identifying our ethnicity in only one way. Any discussion of this topic should allow for multiple interpretations of each student's ethnic identity. Teachers must also be aware that some students may have a hard time determining their ethnicity and might need help.

Traditional arts associated with ethnicity are so plentiful that volumes have been written on the topic. Knitting is prevalent in many groups. Knitters with Norwegian ancestry often incorporate Norwegian designs into their patterns. Mittens may have traditional Lithuanian motifs, and Northwest Coast Salish knitters sometimes make sweaters with images of local sea monsters.

Carving can have ethnic identity as well. TV personality George Lopez, for example, was a sixth-generation *santos* carver from New Mexico. *Santos* carvers, native-born Hispanic artists, produce their own images of holy personages. Elijah Pierce also carves religious imagery—he created painted bas-relief carvings that illustrate Bible stories from an African-American perspective.

Basket makers may be Pomo, Haida, or Nootka, and a knowledgeable viewer can readily distinguish between the baskets of the three tribes. Baskets were (and on some reservations still are) used for hauling loads, winnowing, sifting, storage, and even housing rattlesnakes. African-American baskets created in Mt. Pleasant, South Carolina, are coiled in much the same way they were made hundreds of

3.5 *Inga Schneider, Norwegian knitter. Ashland, Oregon. Photo courtesy of the Randall V. Mills Folklore Archive, University of Oregon.*

Discussion Point

Read the following quote, which is a response to the question "Do you work in the Hispanic community here in Chicago?" Explain why the respondent answered as she did. Pose a similar question to yourself and see if you can respond with similar complexity.

"To which community in particular are you referring, sir? Are you referring to the Mexican community of the West Side or to the Puerto Rican community of West Town? Do you mean the new Central American community in Logan Square or that of the Cuban residents on Milwaukee Avenue? Do you mean, perhaps, to use 'community' in a broader sense and refer to all the countries of South America, Mexico, Central America, and the Caribbean—in which case we should not say Hispanic, because there are those territories, including Brazil, which constitutes one-fifth of South America and was not settled by the Spaniards and therefore is not Hispanic. Or by Hispanic, do you simply refer to the Spanish-speaking? Forty percent of the Guatemalan population doesn't speak Spanish and neither did my Yaqui mother when she came to live here. . . ."

—From Ana Castillo, *Sapogonia* (New York: Doubleday, 1990), 311.

Discussion Point

The locations of Native American ruins are no longer on maps. Why do you think this is? If you were in charge of creating the maps, would you have removed them? Explain the pros and cons of making your decision.

years ago in West Africa. Changes relate mainly to the introduction of pine needles due to the declining growth of sea grasses along the coast.

Mehndi is the East Indian art of decorating women's hands and feet with intricate designs using a mixture of eucalyptus oil and henna. Hmong-embroidered storycloths, created by older women refugees from Laos, tell about life in their homelands before the Vietnam War. Pennsylvania Germans, for many years, made elaborate birth and death records, and some Jews still create beautifully designed wedding contracts.[18]

Expressions of our ethnic visual culture are ubiquitous. We need to pay careful attention to what these objects say about shaping our lives and identities. Once a classroom discussion about ethnicity begins, and children start asking questions at home, new discoveries are easily made.

Other Folklife Points of Origin

Folklife and traditional art are not always old. New forms of tradition are created all the time.

Traditional art may focus on cultural areas other than those already mentioned. For example, folk groups could be individuals who form cultural communities by generation, region, sexual identity, economics, gender, and any other belief system or experience that might bring people together.

As we study folk groups, folklife, and its related folk art and folk speech, we should remember that everyone belongs to many groups at one time, and that visual expressions can hold many meanings among varying folk groups. It is also important to be aware that folklife is dynamic—it changes and adapts to different spaces, times, and needs.

Notes

1 Alan Dundes, *Interpreting Folklore* (Bloomington: Indiana University Press, 1980), 9.

2 Kristin G. Congdon, "The Meaning and Use of Folk Speech in Art Criticism," *Studies in Art Education,* 27, no. 3 (1985): 65-75.

3 Robert Farris Thompson, *Flash of the Spirit* (New York: Vintage Books, 1983), 13–16.

4 Lizabeth A. Cohen, "Embellishing a Life of Labor: An Interpretation of the Material Culture of American Working-Class Homes, 1885–1915," *Journal of American Culture* 3, no. 4 (1980): 752–75.

5 Beverly Hungry Wolf, *The Ways of My Grandmother* (New York: Quill, 1982), 100.

6 Donald M. Lance, "Folk Speech," in *American Folklore: An Encyclopedia,* ed. Jan Harold Brunvand (New York: Garland, 1996), 281.

7 Susan Roach, "The Kinship Quilt: An Ethnographic Semiotic Analysis of a Quilting Bee," in *Women's Folklore, Women's Culture*, eds. Rosan A. Jordan and Susan Kalcik (Philadelphia: University of Pennsylvania Press, 1985), 54–64.

8 Steve Siporin, *American Folk Masters: The National Heritage Fellows* (New York: Abrams, 1992), 119.

9 Larry Calloway, "Atlanta Goings-on Sometimes Come Across as Unprintable," *Albuquerque Journal*, Friday, July 22, 1988, A5.

10 See, for example, Nicholas R. Spitzer, "Cultural Conservation," in *Public Folklore,* eds. Robert Baron and Nicholas R. Spitzer (Washington: Smithsonian Institution Press, 1992), 77–103.

11 Tina Bucuvalas, Peggy A. Bulger, and Stetson Kennedy, *South Florida Folklife* (Jackson: University of Mississippi Press, 1994), 96.

12 Beverly J. Robinson, "Vernacular Spaces and Folklife Studies within Los Angeles' African American Community," in *Home and Yard: Black Folk Life Expressions in Los Angeles* (Los Angeles: California Afro-American Museum, 1987), 19–27.

13 John Michael Vlach, *Back of the Big House* (Chapel Hill: The University of North Carolina, 1993), 34.

14 For information on these environments, see John Beardsley, *Gardens of Revelation* (New York: Abbeville Press, 1995), and Roger Manley and Mark Sloan, *Self-Made Worlds: Visionary Folk Art Environments* (New York: Aperature, 1997).

15 Ormond Loomis, "Buckaroos," in *Webfoots and Bunchgrassers: Folk Art of the Oregon Country,* ed. Suzie Jones (Eugene: University of Oregon Museum of Art, 1980), 86–103.

16 See Kristin G. Congdon, "Occupational Art and Occupational Influences on Aesthetic Preferences: A Democratic Perspective," in *Art in a Democracy,* eds. Doug Blandy and Kristin G. Congdon (New York: Teachers College Press), 110–23.

17 M. J. Gladstone, *A Carrot for a Nose: The Form of Folk Sculpture on America's City Streets and Country Roads*, (New York: Charles Scribner's Sons, 1974), 52.

18 For a discussion on folk art from the folklore perspective, including many ethnic examples, see Kristin G. Congdon, "Art, Folk," in *American Folklore: An Encyclopedia,* ed. Jan Harold Brunvand (New York: Garland, 1996), 46–53.

4

Why Should Art Programs Focus on Community?

The preceding two chapters described how membership in communities is central to the human experience and demonstrated the wide range of folklife and artistic practices associated with communities of many kinds. This chapter will make a case for attending to communities and folklife in education generally, and in art education in particular. As reasons for developing community-based art programs are suggested, they are supported by examples drawn from communities at home and around the world. While not all the examples listed are centered on what a folklorist might call "folklife," they all function to enhance community life.

To Promote Individual and Group Mental Health

One of the main functions of art has always been healing. All over the world and throughout time, art has been used to balance the world, purify the mind, and heal the body. Many religions, for example, celebrate divine statues that have the power to perform miraculous cures. But the power of art to affect individual and group mental health extends beyond the realm of what most of us call religion. A neighborhood that is pleasant to live in is naturally a better place to live than one that is ridden with crime, just as an easy ride to and from work affects how we will behave when we reach our destination.[1]

In the early 1990s, the Five Oaks Neighborhood of Dayton, Ohio, was filled with racial tension and criminal activity. Its buildings were neglected and in decline. In response, the city put in speed bumps and barriers. Streets were closed and logos and signs symbolizing a positive neighborhood view were designed and put up. The neighborhood was divided into smaller community groups, which resulted in people having a better sense of ownership and unity. Crimes got harder to commit, people began taking pride in their neighborhood, and things got better.[2]

In Oregon, landscape architect Paul Morris designs spaces that are healing. He participated in designing the memorial for the victims of the bombing of the federal building in Oklahoma City, and the memorial for the victims of the Columbine High School tragedy. Morris believes that when tragedies such as these happen, people need a space to go to where they can address their emotions and express their support. His ideas are inspired by Maya Lin's Vietnam Veterans Memorial, in Washington, DC, which looks as if it were cut into the landscape. Lin's memorial makes us all powerfully aware of how a carefully designed place can help us heal, both individually and communally. Morris asserts that these constructions "are not static places, but places to come and spend time. Places that tell the story of what happened and where we can go on from there."[3]

Roadside memorials—more everyday examples of art that is made to heal—are ubiquitous around the United States, though in some states they are quickly removed by highway departments. Typically, family

4.1 Impromptu altar for Princess Diana at her death. Winter Park, Florida. Photo by Kristin G. Congdon.

and friends of someone killed in a car accident create these memorials. Most often they consist of crosses decorated with flowers and placed by the side of the road where the crash took place. Many memorials in Kentucky are coded with the nicknames of the dead, while memorials in Louisiana often have the name of the deceased with birth and death dates. In southern Louisiana there is a Latin Catholic influence to the shrines that comes from the French traditions of the Southwest. Shrines are sometimes created for particular saints, as well as scenes of the Stations of the Cross.

Art educators can help students recognize how people from all walks of life can use art and an artistic mind to deal with hardship, tragedy, crime, traffic, and other personal and environmental issues. As we participate in well-thought-out artistic responses to our daily lives, we are able to transform our surroundings, and, as a result, transform the way we feel about our communities and ourselves.

To Promote Multicultural Art Education

Almost everyone agrees that it is important to learn about other cultures. Art educators have embraced multicultural art education for decades.[4] The obvious reason we should learn about other cultures include that learning another way of seeing the world expands our own, giving us more choices of what to enjoy and who we might want to become. This helps us to better understand and relate to our neighbors.

To take a multicultural approach, everyone must acknowledge that whatever cultural groups they come from, they are part of the mix. Every community has diversity. In addition to ethnic differences, there are also differences in religion, occupation, and recreational preferences, among other things. To study Vietnam veterans' jackets and compare them to biker jackets or high school sports jackets would

Discussion Point

The mental health of artists is a much debated issue. Some say the most creative people are typically unbalanced, while others (including many art therapists) say that artists become balanced and healthy by creating art. Ask your students to respond to this question by doing research on specific artists. Can any conclusions be made from what they found?

Discussion Point

The following phrases were spoken by whittlers in southern Indiana. Read them to your students and ask them to explain what the artists meant.

"I'm whittling away the problem."

"I'm carving out an idea now."

"I'm cutting against the grain."

"I'm my own carver now."

"I want to carve a place for myself."

—From Simon J. Bronner, *Chain Carvers: Old Men Crafting Meaning* (Lexington: The University Press of Kentucky, 1985), 95.

The Need for Multiple Models

"We need to look at multiple lives to test and shape our own. Growing up with two talented and very different parents, I have never looked for single role models. I believe in the need for multiple models, so that it is possible to weave something new from many different threads."

—From Mary Catherine Bateson, daughter of anthropologists Margaret Mead and Gregory Bateson, in her book, *Composing a Life* (New York: Plume, 1990), 16.

Discussion Point

Solomon H. Katz, a biological anthropologist from the University of Pennsylvania, made this statement: ". . . as a biological concept, race is no longer a useful concept. In a sense we've outgrown it." Discuss this statement with your students. Ask them: "If race is not biological, is it cultural?" Ask them to explain what kinds of applications the categorization of race has for us today. What uses does it have in the art world?

—Quote is from David L. Wheeler's article, "A Growing Number of Scientists Reject the Concept of Race," *The Chronicle of Higher Education* (February 17, 1995): A8–A10 and A15.

be studying art from a multicultural perspective. In asking how such community expressions are different yet similar, a teacher can help his or her students better understand, and perhaps even celebrate, the significant concepts at the heart of a multicultural approach.

Murals are often made in urban areas to represent the histories of people whose life stories often go untold. To recognize that the history of one person in a city is not always shared by others is to understand that ethnicity makes a difference, but so too do economics, gender, sexual orientation, and age. Sometimes the process of making a mural can bring different groups together in the artistic process. A workbook designed for teenagers leads youth through a series of questions about the cultural artifacts, traditions, and organizations in their communities. Participants are asked questions about local history, crafts, and family members. They are taught how to do fieldwork to document and learn about local customs.

In Scottsdale, Arizona, a diverse group of students ranging from offenders to honor students painted a construction wall. They came together from different backgrounds to depict their anxieties and pleasures related to adolescence. Just as the Greeks, Romans, Chinese, and Mayans painted murals telling their stories, so too do the youth in Scottsdale.[5] These examples demonstrate that our own local world is multicultural. A community-based art program provides opportunities for students to learn, firsthand, the great benefits of living in such a world.

To Recognize and Celebrate Local Customs

Communities become strong by celebrating local customs. Collaborative efforts bring people together to share common beliefs and rituals. In doing so, friendships are made, roots are formed, and identities are reshaped. Over a number of years, the Folk Arts Division of the Michigan State University Museum has sponsored a project called "FolkPatterns" in partnership with Michigan 4-H Youth Programs.[6] This program emphasizes community heritage and identity. Students learn about traditional crafts, foods, and local history with a focus on exploring their own traditions. Lessons might be on exploring gravestone symbols, learning a folk dance, or collecting stories about the weather. Local Michigan customs are made more visible, understood, and valued within the community.

In 1991, Miami Beach resident Gina Cunningham, a certified art teacher, and her husband, Peter Eves, took eleven Haitian boat people into their home. The couple said that the food was great at their house during that time, since their houseguests were good cooks. Spurred by the bad press Haitians were receiving at the time, along with their experiences

Try This

Teachers can read the following quote to their students, asking them to explain what the author means and whether they agree with it or not.

"Our effectiveness in multicultural art education may be enhanced if we continue to question underlying assumptions of art historical scholarship, a necessary first step in freeing ourselves from the grip of a single aesthetic system. Whether we like it or not, art educators are embarked on a process of expansion of our definitions of art and the artist. One part of this process is the development of a critical understanding of our own traditions and their limits; another is the sympathetic study of different aesthetic systems insofar as these are available to us."

—From page 157 of Lynn M. Hart's article "Aesthetic Pluralism and Multicultural Art Education," *Studies in Art Education* 32, no. 3 (1991): 145–59.

4.2 *Haitian mural in Little Haiti, Miami, Florida. Photo by Bud Lee.*

Discussion Point

Ask your students to contemplate the following quote from the American Council for the Arts. Is there any truth to the accusation? If not, should the perception be changed, and what can be done to change it?

"Artists involved with issues of identity are often dismissed as inconsequential, parochial, self-marginalizing, trendy, lacking in intellectual or aesthetic quality, or even by the old cliché, 'not universal,' as if to say it is somehow impossible to make truly significant work based on racial or ethnic identity, no matter how able the artist."

—From Margo Machida, "Arttable: A Panel Discussion: Race, Ethnicity and Culture in the Visual Arts," *Update: American Council for the Arts* 14, no. 2 (March/April 1993): 3–11. Machida is an artist, independent curator, and founding member of Godzilla, an Asian-American Art Network.

with good Haitian food and a love of Haitian art, Cunningham and Eves started a restaurant called TapTap in 1993. The restaurant educates and enlightens people about Haitian culture by providing a place to enjoy great Haitian food, art exhibitions, music, films, and rituals. Artists of all kinds, journalists, and various other community members began to frequent TapTap, asking to learn more about Haiti. As a result, perspectives about Haitians began to change. Gina Cunningham, in essence, was able to make an educational experience out of a restaurant, demonstrating one more way that art promotes learning outside formal educational settings.[7]

Teachers who wish to create community-based art programs in the more formal setting of the school, however, can see from this example how familiarity with the customs of a culture can increase the tendency to value and celebrate them. In the process, students can take pride in, and gain insights into, practices that were once unfamiliar and seemed strange.

In addition to providing insight into other cultures, close examination of local customs can introduce artistic practices that might be "borrowed" and adapted for personal or community use. One wonderful way to study local customs is to look at African-American memory jugs. The tradition comes from the Kongo, where the living commemorate the dead by decorating tombs with embedded glass and porcelain. Robert Farris Thompson calls this work "ceramic drums for the dead." By studying them, students can find out who the commemorated person was and how he or she lived. This tradition has been adapted by people from various cultural traditions who want to make memory jars of an event, a person, or a relationship. Teachers can encourage students to adapt this practice to varying local customs.[8]

To Recognize Local Artists and Artworks

Art study often focuses on artists in major museums while neglecting the art and artists in our communities. Studying works by local artists can provide richness to curricular activities, while making educational activities more meaningful to students and community members.

The Fund for Folk Culture has supported locally based art traditions since 1990. A variety of local traditions have been celebrated and given visibility with support from the National Endowment for the Arts and the Lila Wallace-Reader's Digest Fund, the Pew Charitable Trusts, and other generous contributors. In Dearborn, Michigan, support was given to the Arab Community Center for Economic and Social Services to fund the presentation "A Community Between Two Worlds: Arab Americans in Greater Detroit." This exhibition of traditional arts included instrument making, embroidery, calligraphy, jewelry making, and henna design. Other supported activities include the seventh annual California Indian Basketweavers Gathering in Nevada City, California, and workshops on the preservation of New Mexico's historic adobe churches. These activities recognize, validate, and strengthen locally based customs. Art educators would do well to encourage students to participate in activities such as these and to use projects and programs supported by The Fund for Folk Culture as models for their study.[9]

If an educator develops a curriculum around local customs, local artists and artworks should be included in the plan. However, not all local art and artworks focus on local customs. Some artists like working with local youth or community members, but base their artistic activities on a wider scope of issues or ideas.

Discussion Point

In the early 1970s, Ron Iannone wrote about his experience teaching in the Appalachian Mountains. Because Iannone is a scholar with a Ph.D., he often felt out of place in this context. Read the following quote to the class and lead the class in a discussion about the point Iannone was making. Ask students how the insight described here might teach us all something about our own community and how we think about people and education.

"Today, they [the students] asked me about the camshaft; of course I didn't know one damn thing about it. This surprised them, because they thought everyone with a doctorate should know everything there is to know in this world. . . . I know very little of life after being schooled for something like twenty-two years. After the fellows realized I didn't know anything about the camshaft, they asked Junie, the janitor who also worked in the Boiler Room. . . . He is a beautiful person, open, warm, compassionate, and he has an intuitive understanding of the mountaineer children. While he was explaining the camshaft to the fellows, they were in a trance and gave him their utmost attention and respect. I watched him very carefully and he knew how to explain the complicated mechanism of the camshaft. I think sometimes the more schooling one has the stupider he gets."

—From Ron Iannone, *"School Ain't No Way . . .": Appalachian Consciousness* (Parsons, WV: McClain Printing Company, 1972), 45–46.

Tim Rollins works with teenagers and young adults in his Bronx neighborhood but chooses to focus his collaborative artworks on classic works of literature. This white artist works with African-American and Hispanic students in the South Bronx who have had trouble reading. Since he wants to help them work through difficult and pervasive issues, their reading list includes Paulo Freire's *A Pedagogy of the Oppressed*, Ralph Waldo Emerson's essay "Self-Reliance," Henry David Thoreau's *Walden*, Georges Bataille's *Literature and Evil*, and Tillie Olsen's *Silences*. The group, responding visually in various forms, is collectively called Tim Rollins and KOS, which stands for Kids of Survival, because, they say, the work is about survival. The students learn about life outside the Bronx, and by seeing the work done by Tim Rollins and KOS, those of us who live outside New York City learn about the Bronx.[10] Teachers who want to work in this fashion should consider how this approach strengthens the youth involved and their community, as well as the art world in general.

To Develop an Active Citizenry

Almost everyone understands that a democracy functions best when its citizens are educated and involved. But not everyone understands that art activities can help promote this goal. Because we learned about twentieth-century art by studying the expressions of individual artists in the isolated environment of a museum or gallery, we often neglect to think about how art has the power to connect us and help us think through community-based issues.

In Lyndhurst, New Jersey, the Hackensack Meadowlands Development Commission's Education Center teaches students about trash and what happens to it. Hartford, Vermont, has a similar education center. The Connecticut Resources Recovery

Authority Visitors Center is affectionately called a "garbage museum" because it focuses on educating students about the growing crisis of landfills. These organizations teach about waste reduction, recycling, resources recovery, and ecological sustainability. While these are not necessarily art museums, a growing number of artists are interested in garbage, our responsibility to deal with it in an ecological manner, and our connection to it.[11] Mierle Laderman Ukeles is the self-appointed artist-in-residence in the New York Sanitation Department. Her 1987 installation, *Re-Entry for Flow City*, is a ninety-foot passageway with twenty tons of recyclables, a constructed viewing ramp, and audio providing the visitor with information on waste disposal and related environmental concerns. Ukeles' art projects engage viewers as participants in reconsidering their relationship and responsibility to their waste and how they manage it.[12]

Teachers can encourage students to identify problems in their own communities, such as homelessness, crime, and drugs. Students can use Mierle Laderman Ukeles as a model, appointing themselves as artists to engage audiences to become aware of problems and concerns. Art clearly has the ability to educate and engage people to think about community-based concerns while providing them with a space to help find solutions.

To Promote the Connection between Art and Life

The more one studies the lives of artists, the more one encounters their views on the interconnectedness of life and art. This notion is increasingly evident in contemporary art and serves as a major focus of this book. It is important to reiterate this concept because it is the foundation of community-based art programming.

Try This

Jack Mackie, an artist based in Seattle, sells his ideas to public commissions. On one Seattle project, he worked with civil engineers, an urban design group, and a landscape architect. Together they placed inlaid bronze footsteps in a sidewalk. Looking like foot travelers, they are actually placed in dance-step configurations, including the foxtrot, tango, and waltz.

Ask students to describe the actions of pedestrians as they encounter the artwork. Describe the changes in emotions that might take place in the space. Break the class into small groups and ask them to identify a space in their neighborhood where this kind of artwork might be successful. Give each student a job (landscape designer, dance researcher, urban designer, etc.). Have each group make a plan for a similar kind of project based on a dance they enjoy. Each group might do a presentation to the class or community group.

One example of the connection between art and life can be found in the work of Appalshop Films, based in Whitesburg, Kentucky. Appalshop, founded in 1969, is a prominent art center that makes and distributes films and musical recordings in Appalachia. When art teacher John Gorley wanted to help his students at Dilce Combs High School in Perry County, Kentucky, to see the connection between their heritage and art-making, he showed them three award-winning films produced by Appalshop: *Long Journey Home*, *Coalmining Women*, and *On Our Own Land*. These documentary-film artworks motivated students to make sculptures about life in the coal mines. One of the resulting life-size sculptures depicts eight miners escaping from a cave-in, while another shows a miner dying of black lung disease in a hospital bed.[13]

If teachers educate students about where artists get their inspiration, the students will begin to see how education, place, upbringing, and life experiences influence artists. Teachers can also help by pointing out community-based history and encouraging students to talk to their elders about their lives. In the case of studying coal-mining practices, students might think about what spending so much time underground might be like. They could interview coal miners and ask them to describe their experiences, which might inspire the students to create. If working conditions seem unjust, students can make posters, involving themselves in community-based issues. Teachers could also talk to students about the rescue of the nine Pennsylvania miners in the summer of 2002, and how students could make a film about the event.

To Understand, Celebrate, and Build on Local History

Every community has history that is cause for celebration, and history that is shameful or regrettable in some way. Both extremes are important to keep visible, which is not to be confused with promoting negative history. We need to recognize the best of who we are while we understand that no community is perfect. None of us would want to go back to the days of separate water fountains, waiting rooms, and schools for blacks and whites, but it is important to remember that there was a time when we lived in segregated spaces. When wrongful actions of our history are depicted in artworks, they must be done with respect to the people who were victimized.

In Edwardsville, Illinois, a public art mural was placed on the façade of the new city hall building in 1967. It depicted the town's history, complete with the figure of a freed slave. Twenty years later, the African-American community objected and asked that it be removed. They did not object to the fact that a freed slave had been part of the mural, but they were angry about the way in which he had been portrayed. The image, African-Americans claimed, was in the disrespectful, "Stepin Fetchit tradition."[14] Stepin Fetchit was an African-American character actor of the 1920s and '30s whose name became synonymous with degrading racial stereotypes. Teachers can help students with sensitive issues by doing group critiques of artworks with diverse groups of people. We can learn from others how images can become stereotypical and demeaning.

In July 1998, children participating in a summer camp at Lauer's Park Elementary School in Reading, Pennsylvania, researched local history to find out what well-known people had visited their community. They painted a passenger train on the side of a building, and in the windows depicted the famous visitors, including Babe Ruth; Charles Duryea, the first person to make a car in the United States; and Jack Johnson, the first African-American heavyweight champion boxer. Everyone agreed that this project gave the children—and hopefully other community members—an appreciation for their neighborhood and its history.[15]

To Interact Positively with the Environment

Teaching children and youth to care about their neighborhoods is a goal that is becoming increasingly important. In downtown Philadelphia, a remarkable program in the early 1990s put former graffiti writers to work painting murals over walls they had previously trashed. The program, called the Anti-Graffiti Network, has been a huge success, transforming a run-down community into an art gallery. Project director Jane Golden said the youth who participate in creating the murals come out of the program with improved self-esteem, strong values, and a sense of responsibility about their place in the world.[16]

Playgrounds are being designed today to encourage children not only to focus on physical activity, but also to exercise their imagination. Some of these playgrounds teach about physics, the environment, local history, and geography. Deborah Ryan from the University of North Carolina at Charlotte has partnered with children, mostly from poor neighborhoods, to design three playgrounds. They used discarded and recycled materials such as sewer pipes in an effort to give value and use to objects that have been devalued. She asserts that the extension of this idea is to elevate the children and neighborhoods that have been devalued. Each place is interactive and created in such a way that it encourages children to explore and create.[17]

Try This

Most folklorists believe that traditional art must be studied along with the life and work of the artist. By studying it in this manner, local history is taught and understood. Identify two or three local artists who do traditional artwork and invite them to visit your classroom. Ask the artists to talk about their artwork, how they learned it, and how it functions. After they have gone, engage your students in a discussion to see what they have learned about local history.

Discussion Point

Folklorist Gregory Hansen reported that in South Central Indiana artists are now painting sheep. He explained that there is a tradition there of using paint to mark wool that has been graded, but now sheep are being painted with all kinds of designs including pumpkins and scarecrows for Halloween, turkeys and pilgrims for Thanksgiving, and of course, Santa Claus for Christmas. Teachers can ask students how they feel about this practice. Are there other practical reasons for painting sheep? Does it harm the animal? What kinds of designs might your students suggest for sheep in Indiana or other areas of the country?

—From a discussion with Gregory Hansen

An impressive example of how art has been used to preserve and develop an entire town comes from Eatonville, Florida, the oldest incorporated African-American municipality in the United States, and hometown of Zora Neale Hurston, the famous folklorist, anthropologist, and writer. In the late 1980s, this small town was slated to have its main road widened to a four-lane highway. Realizing that this large roadway would severely damage the cohesiveness of the town, N. Y. Nathiri established Preserve the Eatonville Community, Inc. (P.E.C.), to educate others about the importance of this town and why it

4.3 *Stilt walker at the 1994 Zora Neale Hurston Festival of the Arts and Humanities. Eatonville, Florida. Photo by Kristin G. Congdon.*

should be preserved and celebrated as an important historic place. The first annual Zora Neale Hurston Festival for the Arts took place in January 1989. Tens of thousands of visitors come each year, and in the late 1990s the town was placed on the National Register of Historic Places. Each year the festival gets bigger, drawing people from around the world. The road through town remains, at this writing, a two-lane highway.[18]

The above examples show how community members who participate in the betterment of their communities through art activities are able to establish their neighborhoods as better places to live. Teachers and students can keep files on other communities that have successfully changed their environments through artistic activity.

To Expand on the Aesthetic Dimensions of One's Life

One of the most exciting things to happen with the increased interest in community-based art is that we are now paying attention to more objects that have aesthetic value. Many of these objects are making their way into art exhibitions, which, in turn, prompts us to pay more attention to them in their original contexts.

In 1987, for example, the John Michael Kohler Arts Center in Sheboygan, Wisconsin, coordinated an exhibition of Wisconsin's traditional art. The exhibition and catalog were titled *From Hardanger to Harleys: A Survey of Wisconsin Folk Art*. Included were hardanger (a Norwegian form of embroidery), Harley-Davidson motorcycles, African-American walking canes, a woven Czechoslovakian wheat cross, handmade picnic baskets, Latvian knitted mittens, Hmong traditional customs, handmade marker buoys, duck decoys, and an Amish double rocker. Many states have done survey exhibitions of this

Delight in the Things We See and Touch

"The handmade object satisfies a need no less imperative than hunger and thirst: the need to take delight in the things we see and touch, whatever their everyday uses."

—From Octavio Paz, *Convergences: Essays on Art and Literature* (San Diego: Harcourt Brace Jovanovich, 1987), 58–59.

kind that result in our paying more careful attention to the aesthetics in our everyday life. Art teachers can give the same kind of recognition to everyday art objects by placing them in the curriculum, thereby expanding on the range of objects we pay attention to aesthetically and from which we can derive pleasure.[19]

The reasons for developing art programs that are rooted in community-based traditions are many. They encourage us to recognize and celebrate local customs and local artists and their work. These programs help develop an active citizenry and promote a connection between art and life as they help us understand and build on local history. Students involved in community-based art programming are encouraged to interact positively with the environment and expand on the aesthetic dimensions of their lives.

These are all sound educational goals, many of which could be noted as goals in other academic disciplines. Each goal is intended to assist us to better understand our natural and built environment as we interact with it, represent it, and work to change it for the better. By looking and acting locally, students in community-based art programs are better able to understand the impulses and practices within communities around the world.

Notes

1   For more information on art and mental health, read Michael Brenson's article, "Healing in Time," in Mary Jane Jacob's anthology *Culture in Action: A Public Art Program of Sculpture Chicago* (Seattle: Bay Press, 1995), 16–49. To learn more about how the discipline of art therapy can benefit by emphasizing mental health rather than mental illness, see Kristin G. Congdon, "Normalizing Art Therapy," *Art Education* 43, no. 3, 1990: 18–24 and 41–43.

2   See Ellis Cose, "Drawing up Safer Cities," *Newsweek* (July 11, 1994): 57.

3   For more information on Paul Morris's work, see Debra Gwartney, "Healing by Design," in *Old Oregon: News of UO Alumni* 80, no. 2 (Winter 2000): 35–36.

4   Two of the most prominent art educators who spent their careers developing theoretical foundations for multicultural art education are June King McFee and F. Graeme Chalmers. Their publications are numerous and can be found in *Art Education* and *Studies in Art Education*.

5   For more information on painting murals with youth, see Samuel Greengard, "The Big Picture," in *Teaching Tolerance* 3, no. 1 (Spring 1994): 50–55.

6   Workbook may be obtained by writing: Cooperative Extension Service, Michigan State University, East Lansing, MI 48824.

7   There were others who worked with Gina Cunningham and Peter Eves to start TapTap. It has now changed ownership, but the restaurant continues to be a hotspot for Haitian art and culture. Visitors can enjoy murals, music, food, and art at 819 5th St., Miami Beach, FL 33162. A "taptap" is any brightly painted vehicle that is privately owned, runs regular routes, and serves as a public bus. Information on TapTap comes from personal communication with Gina Cunningham on August 27, 1999, and November 29, 2000.

8   For more information on memory jugs and for the quote in this paragraph, see the small book titled, *Forget-Me-Not: The Art & Mystery of Memory Jugs*. The Foreword is by Robert Farris Thompson and essays are by Brooke Davis Anderson and Linda Beatrice Brown.

This is a catalog for an exhibition at Diggs Gallery, May 31–August 31, 1996. Brooke Davis Anderson was the curator. The catalog can be purchased through Diggs Gallery at Winston-Salem State University, 601 Martin Luther King, Jr., Drive, Winston-Salem, NC 27110.

9   For a report on these programs, contact The Fund for Folk Culture, P.O. Box 1566, Santa Fe, NM 87504-1566 (e-mail: folkfund@aol.com).

10   Many articles have been written about Tim Rollins and KOS. Good information on how they function can be found in the chapter titled "Tim Rollins and KOS: The Amerika Series" by Marcia Wallace in her book, *Invisibility Blues: From Pop to Theory* (New York: Verso, 1990), 199–210.

11   Information on these organizations comes from Elizabeth Ross, "Garbage Museum Aims to Change Wasteful Ways," *Christian Science Monitor*, September 21, 1993, 10–11.

12   For more information on her work, see the artist's article, "A Journey: Earth/City/Flow" in *Art Journal* 51, no. 2 (1992): 12–14.

13   To contact Appalshop Educational Services, write them at 306 Madison Street, Whitesburg, KY 41858 or call them at (606) 633-0108. The report on John Gorley's students was found in a resource section of *Teaching Tolerance* 5, no. 1 (1996): 57.

14   For more on this controversy, see Sylvia Hochfield, "The Moral Rights (and Wrongs) of Public Art," *Artnews* 87, no. 5 (1988): 143–46.

15   Mary Young, "Campers Track 6th Ward History," *Reading Eagle/Reading Times* (July 30, 1998): B1 and B2.

16   See Steven Barboza, "A Mural Program to Turn Graffiti Offenders Around," *Smithsonian* 24, no. 4 (July 1993): 63–70.

17   Jean Seligmann and Alden Cohen, "New Grounds for Child's Play," *Newsweek,* November 1, 1993: 68B and 68D.

18   The author writes as a participant in each year's planning of the festival, which is now the Zora Neale Hurston Festival of the Arts and Humanities.

19   The catalog for the Wisconsin folk-art exhibition can be obtained by contacting the John Michael Kohler Arts Center, Sheboygan, WI 53082-0489.

Art Programs Focusing on the
Natural and Built Environment

When thinking about community-based art programs, the first thing that comes to most people's minds is the art-making that occurs in their own neighborhoods. Neighborhoods are generally defined as places with a recognizable natural and built environment. Neighborhood communities are usually subdivisions of cities and towns, unless the town is quite small. Residents typically know where the boundaries are. Often neighborhoods have parks, places of worship, schools, and community centers where people gather and make local decisions that affect the quality of their lives. All too often, these decisions are made by people with little consideration for the plants and animals that also live there. Historical buildings, which remind us of the roots of our identity, are also often neglected in the name of progress.

Some theorists believe that our traditional anthropocentric approach to community should be reconfigured in ways that emphasize our interdependence with our environment.[1] From this point of view, community decisions would include plans that respect the health of waterways, plants, animals, birds, and even insects, along with the humans who call the area home. It would mean paying attention to historical buildings and sacred spaces. Shared spaces would be given the same consideration as individual ones. Artists, especially those who care about tradition, are already making these kinds of connections. For example, loggers are often good wood carvers, and Native American basket makers are generally knowledgeable about local grasses, roots, and bark. Many artists look for ways that their art can relate to the environment. Andy Goldsworthy, for instance, uses only materials he finds in the environment, and Ana Mendieta imposed her body in the earth to create a dialogue between the female body and the landscape.

Although all people and all communities have a value-driven relationship with their natural and built environment, these relationships vary. Much depends on how we define "nature" and "community." What we understand to be nature has a great deal to do with our diverse cultural histories.[2] Artists, like all people, build on their understandings of what community is, based on their individual and cultural experiences.

This chapter will look at some artworks and art programs that relate, in various ways, to the natural and built communities we live in. Ways that art educators can build their own programs and curricula based on these models will be suggested. These projects may not all be folkloric in that they are often initiated by academically trained artists using contemporary theory other than folklore. Still, each of the examples given here may be looked at from a folkloric perspective in that they are rooted in tradition, are community based, or are collaborative in their creation and in the way they function in their local communities. The collaboration, in some cases, may be with nonhumans. Art educators may find this approach to collaboration a bit unusual, but it will help to promote creative thinking and open students' minds to the environment around them.

5.1 Marion Bowers making a Seminole basket. Brighton Reservation, Florida, 1981. Photo by Merri McKenzie. Courtesy of the Florida Folklife Programs, Division of Historical Resources.

Houston's Project Row Houses

Some contemporary artists use a particular space in their communities as the foundation for their art-work. Teachers can use these artists as models for building curricula. This encourages students to explore local history that has community-based meanings. Students also learn how to be activists in their own neighborhoods, making changes for a better quality of life.

Coordinated by artist Rick Lowe, Project Row Houses is a collaborative, community-based project located in one of Houston's historical African-American neighborhoods. The project began with a conversation among several of the city's African-American artists who were interested in establishing a positive creative force in their community. Their site became a block of twenty-two shotgun-style houses[3] in a neighborhood with deep cultural and historical roots dating back to the Civil War. The houses were purchased and restored, and the reno-vated buildings are now used as galleries, studios, and homes for single parents. Each artist is given a house to restore in a way that will speak to issues relevant to the African-American community. The Young Mothers Residential Program not only pro-vides housing for families, but encourages residents to be an integral part of the creative community.

This block of homes represents a communal and cooperative way of living that is reflective of the tra-ditional African-American community, especially in the South. Numerous local organizations have pro-vided funding, including businesses, foundations, and the National Endowment for the Arts. Participants have pulled weeds and planted gardens, built playgrounds, helped to repair the houses, and have been involved in other diverse ways.[4]

Saving Cultural History

"When I read that we lose 15,000–20,000 species of plants and animals a year through the logging, ranching and min-ing that escalates rainforest destruction, my mind immediately begins to ponder how to possibly calculate the number of songs, myths, words, ideas, artifacts, techniques—all the cultural knowledge and practices lost per year in . . . mega-diversity zones."

—Steven Feld, who writes about the rainforest in Papua New Guinea

Discussion Point

Vicki Meek and Tracy Hicks, two artists
who worked with Project Row Houses,
based their work on the oral histories of
neighborhood elders. Cameras were distributed to people in the neighborhood
with the idea of capturing "things worth
preserving." These photos were placed in
rows of glass jars as if they were "pre-
serves on a shelf." The dialogue that
occurred with audience members was
viewed as important. Why do you think
it was important? If you were to recreate this project in your own community, what kinds of pictures would you
take?

*Classroom Connections: Building
Neighborhoods as Art*

The Project Row Houses provide a useful model for
thinking about possible projects, both large and
small, in any community. Educators might point to
the project as an example of artistic practices that
help people to expand their ideas about art.
Teachers might engage students in discussions about
this project and how it is similar to, and different
from, other "products" typically produced by artists.
Understanding how art processes are changing in
contemporary times might be difficult for students
who have the idea that art is mostly about painting
and sculpture. Shifting students' focus
to the creative process will help the conversation
have depth.

Asking the following questions will help create a
dialogue about the artwork and how it might trans-
fer to one's own community:

*5.2 "Fashion as Metaphor" by Selven O'Keef Jarmon, Project Row
Houses, Houston, Texas, 1996. Photo courtesy of Project Row
Houses. Installation exploring fashion as silent drama.*

- What exactly is the artwork produced by Project Row Houses? Is it the houses or the work done in them?
- Can the renovators be called artists?
- How about the people who work on the gardens?
- Does this program provide any new ways of thinking about art?

As students contemplate these interesting philosophical questions associated with Project Row Houses, they might be asked to reexamine their beliefs about art. As they share their ideas and explain their reasons for holding them, they can more readily see how they, too, can be involved in art projects that address their own community.

To help students consider the possibility of engaging in a similar activity at home, ask: What kinds of traditional neighborhoods do you have in your city/town? What are its historical and cultural roots? Who can help you find this information? How does the natural and built environment reflect this history and culture? What aspects of the community are now hidden and worth making visible? How could an artist or a group of artists help renew these cultural aspects by making them more visible? Who needs to be involved?

Students can make a visual plan explaining their ideas. Completed plans can be displayed in the classroom, in a public community space, or on a website. By engaging in this process, students gain new information about the ever-changing nature of art. Suggest that art is not just about objects that can be bought and sold, framed, and moved from place to place. Students see instead that art can be about making a neighborhood a better place to live. The curriculum can be designed around ecological issues, local history, and ways of engaging an active citizenry.

5.3 "Loss of Innocence" by Natalie Lovejoy, Project Row Houses, Houston, Texas, 1997. Photo courtesy of Project Row Houses. Installation dealing with incest.

Discussion Point

Folklorist Gregory Hansen reports that he was talking to a sheep farmer in south central Indiana who told him about sheep painting. The farmer reported that he was using paint to mark wool that had been graded, and that he had recently begun to employ an artist to do the markings. The artist began painting the sheep with all kinds of designs, including nude women. When the farmer discovered this, he told the artist that he couldn't paint nude women on the sheep because he was a deacon in a church just down the road and church members wouldn't approve. Reportedly, the nude women were repainted with bikinis. Fortunately for the farmer, the artist had also painted designs and some holiday motifs.

How do you feel about the painted sheep? Is this a good idea or a bad one? Can you name other countries where sheep are painted? What is the purpose of sheep painting in those countries? [Answer: In Ireland they are painted to denote who they belong to.] If you were to paint an animal in your community, what would it be and why would you paint it? What kinds of designs would you use on the animals and why?

Cumberland County's Folk Artists in Education Program

Artists in Education Programs have been in schools for decades. These partnerships can be very successful when an artist works closely with a teacher to develop curriculum that fits into the goals of the art program. When the curriculum is integrated with other disciplines, the learning process is extended and the potential for learning about art and other subjects is enhanced.

In Cumberland County, New Jersey, in the 1980s, the goal of the Folk Artists in Education Program (FAIE) was to involve community educators, or folk artists, with teachers to develop coursework that could be integrated into specific grade levels and subject areas. The idea was to share family narratives, customs, and material culture inside the scope of the school. For example, teachers explored ways that knitting could be integrated with math, the ecology of local bodies of water with science, and language with local legends.

More than twenty folk artists participated. The diversity of the participating artists reflected the diversity of the county. Participants included people who came from families who fished, trapped, hunted, farmed, and shucked oysters. Visual artists were experts in painting, embroidery, quilting, jewelry making, and origami.

Photographs of oyster-shucking houses were brought in and discussed. A community member told stories about what work was like in these buildings in the 1920s. He explained how African-Americans would sing spirituals and how that helped them tolerate the hard work and difficult life. Similar discussions took place that focused on other historical buildings, helping students see the connection between who we are, what we do, and how our ancestors and neighbors before us related to the same, yet changing, environment.

From quilters, students learned how quilts were made when thread and cloth weren't readily available. From a seaman, they learned what made a good oyster boat, and from a fisherman they learned to tie traditional knots.

Some visitors were collectors. One resident brought in his arrowheads and explained the art of carving and hunting with the objects, as well as how the carvers and hunters expressed a cultural and historical connection to the land.[5]

Students in Cumberland County began to see how people and art change with the times. They also learned how to read their environment and explain its significance in terms of individual and community identity.

Classroom Connections: Seeing the Past and Designing for the Future

Every community has educators or folk artists who can assist younger residents in learning about the history and culture of their home places. Students can help identify these people, invite them into the classroom, and ask them to guide them in seeing a building or a landscape in a new way. Students can also identify places, occupations, or other aspects of their environment that they are interested in learning more about.

Artists, city planners, and all kinds of businesspeople need to be able to envision change, while at the same time respecting the past. Curriculum can be built around this goal by presenting lessons that teach students to understand the historical functions of the natural and built environment. Sometimes this is difficult for students, especially when they are young and have no experience in historical ways of using a space. Older community members can make a particular kind of history come alive if they are good presenters or storytellers. Programs that moti-

vate students to recognize the importance of the past while designing for the future will enable the participants to provide meaningful solutions to difficult issues that face every community.

There are many ways to help students understand and value a community's history. Expand or modify the following suggestions to address your own local community:

- Have students select a building, like a functioning oyster-shucking house, to relate a select group of residents to the local land or waterways. Students might redesign the building based on how they think it might need to change in the next twenty-five years. In a large group discussion, they should explain their design changes.

- Encourage students to talk to longtime residents in their community. Following the conversations, students might draw a picture of how the residents described a downtown area when they were the students' age. Students might also do research to see how close they came to how it really appeared. In explaining the differences, try to help students to see that there is a difference between lived memories and documented facts. Students might draw pictures of how they see the same downtown area. They might draw a third picture based on how they would like it to be, saving selected older parts that have disappeared. Students should be able to explain their choices.

- Based on interviews with local residents, students might draw maps indicating where the most important areas of their community or town activity were at the beginning of the 1950s, '60s, '70s, '80s, '90s, and now. They might illustrate what functions happened in these places, identify the changes that have taken place, and offer possible reasons for those changes. Finally they might draw a map indicating where they think the most important areas of their community or town activity should be in the future.

These kinds of projects ask students to engage in challenging problem-solving processes. They demonstrate to students how art-making often takes a great deal of research and hard work before one even begins the art product. When curriculum is designed to teach students to research, problem solve, and create artwork, the outcome can give depth to the educational experience. When teachers in other disciplines get involved, students can begin to see how art need not be separate from other areas of study, or from our daily lives.

The Findhorn Foundation

There are some amazing places in our world where things happen that can't easily be explained. Everyone likes to hear about these places, partly because they engage us in trying to find explanations. Often these places are cared for in extraordinary ways. Including these curious places in the curriculum can present students with models for taking care of their own natural and built environment. Findhorn, Scotland, which is set up as a foundaton, is one such intriguing and cared for place.

While the Findhorn Foundation has no formal doctrine or creed, they have a formal statement of purpose: "The Findhorn Foundation is an international spiritual community of around 200 people located in the Northeast of Scotland. The Community was founded in 1962 by Peter and Eileen Caddy and Dorothy Maclean in the belief that humanity is engaged in a planetary expansion of global consciousness, creating new patterns of civilisation infused with spiritual values."[6]

An idea that Findhorn heavily promotes is that growing things and creating art belong together.

Therefore, if you were to visit the community, you would find lots of shrine-like spaces in gardens and around homes. Areas all over the community are taken care of as if they were places to meditate. As a visitor, you are able to see the small things because attention is brought to windowsills, tree roots, stones, mounds of earth, and walking trails. There is an emphasis on the nonhuman world and how that world connects with the health and creativity of humans. When a vegetable garden is planned, it is done in a sustainable way. When trees are used for building, they are taken in a manner that is respectful of the integrity of the forest and promotes the revitalization of the ecosystem. The Findhorn Foundation receives ideas on how to make the quality of life better for all living things from people all over the world.

Classroom Connections:
Making Your Neighborhood Special

The Findhorn Foundation is continually working on programs related to the education and development of creating sustainable communities. Artists are seen as central to this endeavor. Teachers and students might explore this goal in the following ways:

- Students might be asked to think about their own community and prepare a design for a house, school, or community center. Students might consider the plants, animals, and landscape of the area and what kinds of needs they may have. Teachers might invite a naturalist and an architect to the class to aid in this endeavor. This could be an opportunity for an art teacher to collaborate with a science teacher to help students learn about local plants and animals.

- Teachers and students might work together to consider ways to transform places that have become eyesores. Such neglected community spaces could include vacant houses, the edge of a parking lot, or part of the school. After identifying a place that has deteriorated, students can design an artwork that transforms the space into one that people would be drawn to, thereby enhancing their community.

These activities would help challenge the idea that extraordinary places are somewhere other than where we all live. They demonstrate to students that anyplace can be special if people care about it and take actions to make it thrive. Curriculum based on this idea not only helps students see how they can participate in developing spaces that ecologically thrive, it can also help them to see how art can be a part of that process.

Try This

Kevin Orth is a Chicago artist who believes that you can make art out of anything. Many of his art pieces are shrines made out of recycled jars, bottles, light bulbs, flower pots, jar lids, and other materials he finds by scavenging around the neighborhood where he works. After assembling and painting the items with bright colors, the finished sculptures, often called bottle shrines, are placed on boxes and old suitcases that function as pedestals. Sometimes, he quietly returns the finished artworks back to the neighborhoods where he first found the tossed-out items. His choice of materials is practical, but it also involves a deep sense of moral and spiritual obligation. Can you explain how he views his actions as moral and spiritual? Can you identify a section of your community that could use a few bottle shrines? Act on this need.

5.4 *Findhorn, Scotland. Photo by Kristin G. Congdon. An open space made special.*

Graveyards and the Eugene Masonic Cemetery Association

While graveyards might conjure up stories about ghosts and difficult issues of dying, they are also places that can be used to build exciting and meaningful curricula. Before engaging in activities related to graveyards, consider the cultural values of your community. Parents might be asked to understand that art students are exploring graveyards to learn about art, artists, and community-based practices.

Every community has graveyards and burial traditions. Many stonecutters are good artists and their works can be seen in local cemeteries. The older the town, the more opportunity one has to explore local history, especially in a graveyard. Most early stonecutters, especially those from New England, had their own style, which can be recognized with some careful study.[7]

Early materials used in the Northeast United States were varied. They included native slate, marble, soapstone, and fieldstones of every kind. Some gravestones were even made from slate brought over from England or Wales. The type of stone being used influenced the kind of carving that was done. For example, carving in slate resulted in sharp contours and flat planes, whereas carving into marble produced a more rounded relief.[8]

While older New England gravestones and burial practices mostly reflect Anglo rituals and beliefs, other ethnic burial traditions can be easily identified. For example, African-Americans in the South often embellished their gravesites using practices that date back to West Africa. From the beginning of slavery until the early 1900s, it was common practice to place everyday objects belonging to the deceased on the grave. It was believed that these objects would be used by the spirit of the deceased. Sometimes the objects were broken before being placed on the grave to break the chain of bad luck.[9] All cultural groups have ways of interacting with and changing the graveyard landscape when loved ones die. There are variations, of course, even within cultural groups. Some people place fences around the graves while others place photographs, metals, lace, and religious symbols on the grave or gravestone. Studying these sites and the ways in which the dead are honored and memorialized can tell us a great deal about history, culture, and identity.

In Eugene, Oregon, the Eugene Masonic Cemetery is recognized as a primary depository for local history, art, biology, and culture. An association has been formed to study and preserve this site where thousands of European-American emigrants were buried in the mid-nineteenth century. By the 1970s vandalism, mismanagement, and the overgrowth of nonnative plants had plagued the cemetery and community members wanted to restore both the ecological and artistic heritage. The Eugene Masonic Cemetery Association includes historic preservationists, landscape architects, native plant specialists, stoneworkers, and numerous other volunteers. The organization's goal is to turn the cemetery into a multi-use, community-based site that is a refuge for native plants and animals as well as an educational site where art, history, culture, and biology are taught.[10] Increasing support and energy continues to go into this project.

Classroom Connections: The Graveyard as Art

Gravestones and graveyard cultural practices generally relate to ethnic and religious traditions. Also influential are historical practices in a particular area, the availability of land, and water levels. In New Orleans, people must be buried in tombs or vaults aboveground because the water table is so high.

Students can learn a lot about their community and their natural environment by visiting a local cemetery. Teachers might develop a unit that helps students understand community identity, religious practices, and aesthetic values. The following questions might be asked during a visit to a local cemetery:

- How early are the dates on the gravestones?
- Does the artwork (styles, symbols, techniques, materials, etc.) change as the dates change?
- How are the gravestones arranged?
- Are the gravesites planned or randomly dispersed?
- What else is left at the site?
- How do the gravesites and plants relate to each other?
- Is the site cared for? How?
- What has changed over time?
- What kinds of religious and ethnic practices can be identified?
- What can you learn about local living community members by studying how they bury their dead?

Discussion Point

Have you seen roadside memorials or shrines in your community? Who do you think makes them and why are they created? What are they made from? What kinds of laws do you have in your area regarding roadside memorials? Do you agree with these laws or not? Do you know any legends about people who have died along the road? Can you tell them?

Try This

Many kinds of materials have been used for gravestones. The Smithsonian's Museum of Natural History lists the following materials that have been used for markers: wood, cement, metal, stone, granite, marble, slate limestone, and fieldstone. Can you identify these materials in graveyards in your community? Describe the shapes. Are they tablet, tablet-like, vertical slab, obelisk, block, triangular block, horizontal slab, pulpit, figural, sarcophagus, cenotaph, or some other shape or function? Do research on the shapes of these markers. Draw each one and list places where each shape has been used as a gravestone.

5.5 Roadside motorcycle grave near Truches, New Mexico. Photo by Peter Schreyer.

Consider the following projects:

Using the Eugene Masonic Cemetery Association as a model, plan an educational brochure of a local cemetery. Students might explain what visitors can learn about their local history by looking at the gravestones and plant life. They might address the following questions:

- What lessons can be learned about how your community has changed?
- What is valued by studying the cemetery?
- Is there evidence of any traditions related to gender, economic class, occupation, or ethnic identification?

The completed brochure might be distributed to members of the community through local community centers or other groups.

Students might document gravestones by doing rubbings, taking photographs, and creating drawings and maps. In group discussions, they might explain what they have discovered about a cemetery and what they think they have learned. Invite a few long-time community residents to look over students' findings and describe how they might interpret the cemetery's culture and history by looking at the students' visual notes. Students might then compare and contrast the interpretations, refining their original conclusions.

Graveyard projects help to change students' conceptions of the cemetery from a place that you might think about only at Halloween to a place that holds artistic and historical information. Directing their attention to the ways in which graveyards are built and cared for in a community can help students interpret their environment in ways that can enhance their understanding of the various approaches we take to both life and death. These are important topics for any artist.

Lynne Hull and Art for Animals

Lynne Hull is an artist based in Fort Collins, Colorado, who makes art for animals. She worked with local residents in Northern Ireland to help restock salmon in a river by etching images of salmon on basalt boulders that were then placed in fast-flowing sections of the Colin River. These indentations formed resting-places and spawning pools for the fish. In other places, she has planted trees, or made tree-like structures to encourage birds to nest when their natural nesting places had been destroyed.

Reservoir Tree is an environmental sculpture Hull created in Carsinton Water, Derbyshire, England. Although her tree is a human-made sculpture, it clearly functions like a real tree in that it serves as a wildlife habitat. In the summer of 1996, Lynne Hull worked with a team of educators, artists, and naturalists to create an environment for a newly created wetlands area in back of an elementary school outside Columbus, Ohio. Participants made a tall roosting place for birds and many small resting places for dragonflies. The needs of turtles, fish, and ducks also were considered in the ways that the wetlands area was manipulated with new plantings and bundles of interwoven sticks. After the project was completed, students went to the redesigned wetlands to draw the bugs and animals that came to play and live in and around the sculptures and new plantings.[11]

Classroom Connections: Artists as Ecologists

Most everyone's community has been negatively affected by some kind of neglect—overgrowth of nonnative plants, acid rain, garbage, overdevelopment, or worse. The destructive effects of these changes are widespread because when one part of an ecosystem is affected, the balance of the entire system is altered. For example, the loss of trees means the loss of nesting places for birds, oxygen for

Try This

Identify a place outside your school or community building that could attract birds or animals. Discuss what kinds of homes, space, and places are needed for the birds and animals you might be able to attract. Research how they live. Build a sculpture for animals that is both pleasing for you to look at and attractive to the birds or animals you have targeted. Watch and see what happens. If you have been successful, draw a picture of your success.

Discussion Point

Gregg A. Schlanger, a sculptor and art professor from Tennessee, is concerned about the decline of the salmon population in the Pacific Northwest. In 1998 he began making plans to place 100,000 aluminum fish sculptures along 900 miles of the Columbia, Snake, and Salmon Rivers. The artworks will follow the spawning route of the Redfish Lake sockeye salmon and will remain in place for three months. What do you think the response to this installation will be? Can it change the decline of the salmon population? How? Can you think of a similar project that could be done in your community? What steps would you need to take to carry it out?

rvoir Tree, *by Lynne Hull, Carsinton Water, Derbyshire,*
1994. Photo by James Milne.

humans, roots to prevent erosion, and aesthetic beauty and shade. Artists can participate in reversing negative trends by constructing new and different kinds of sculpture that assists in rebalancing the environment. Teachers can develop curriculum projects that assist students in thinking systemically about how artists change the environment, both positively and negatively.

Here are some additional projects worth considering:

Students might research endangered plants and animals in their community. They can discover the environmental changes that have contributed to the endangerment, and discuss how an artist might create an environment where the endangered plants or animals might thrive. Students can discuss the kinds of expertise they would need to help create this environment. Such a project could serve as a catalyst for considering whether or not this act or creation can be considered an artwork. If possible, students should be encouraged to act on their plans.

Students might study the work of other artists who have worked with environmental issues. These artists include Joseph Beuys, Cai Guo-Qiang, Mel Chin, Agnes Denes, Andy Goldsworthy, Hans Haacke, Helen Mayer Harrison and Newton Harrison, Ellen Lanyon, Ana Mendieta, Viet Ngo, Buster Simpson, Mierle Laderman Ukeles, and Meg Webster, among others. As students learn about these artists, they might be asked to consider which artists draw on cultural traditions and community collaboration to do their work. Students might consider these examples as new models for doing artwork. Encourage students to use one or more of these artists' approaches to make a plan that interacts positively with a part of their own community's natural or built environment.

These activities help the student think of art as having consequences. It also demonstrates to them that artists can, and sometimes do, collaborate with scientists, making art and science more closely aligned than we usually tend to think they are. Curricular activities based on the natural and built environment engage students in their physical neighborhoods, encouraging change that enhances the quality of life, not just for human beings, but for the plant and animal life that inhabit the spaces as well. Educators who build curricular units that ad-dress environmental issues produce students who have skills to engage in their communities in ecologically sound ways.

Notes

1 See for example, Laurie Anne Whitt and Jennifer Daryl, "Communities, Environments and Cultural Studies," in *Cultural Studies* 8, no. 1 (1994): 5–31, where the authors emphasize decision making that takes into account community needs that are other than human. They stress the importance of shared circumstances and interests in building community unity.

2 See Giovanna DiChiro in the chapter "Nature as Community: The Convergence of Environment and Social Justice" in *Uncommon Ground: Rethinking the Human Place in Nature*, ed. W. Cronin (New York: W. W. Norton, 1996), 298–320. DiChiro points out that experience with the land is very different for Native Americans, European settlers, enslaved Africans, and indentured Chinese laborers, for example.

3 As explained in chapter 3, shotguns are long, narrow houses, through which one might fire a shot that would enter via the front entrance and exit directly through the back door without doing any damage. The form of the building has been traced back to West Africa.

4. Project Row Houses is located at 2500 Holman, Houston.

5 For a complete description of this ten-year project, see Moonsammy, Rita Zorn, *Passing It On: Folk Artists and Education in Cumberland County, New Jersey* (Trenton: New Jersey State Council on the Arts, 1992).

6 *The Findhorn Foundation: Programs and Workshops October 1998 to April 1999.* (Cluny Hill College, Forres IV36 ORD, Scotland), 3.

7 Avon Neal, "Early New England Gravestones," in *How to Know American Folk Art*, ed. Ruth Andrews (New York, E. P. Dutton, 1977), 15–32.

8 Jean Lipman, *American Folk Art in Wood, Metal and Stone* (Meriden, CT: Meriden Gravure, 1948), 174.

9 Regina A. Perry, "Black American Folk Art: Origins and Early Manifestations," in *Black Folk Art in America 1930–1980*, eds. Jane Livingston and John Beardsley (Jackson: University of Mississippi Press, 1982), 25–37.

10 For more information on The Eugene Masonic Cemetery Association see Kristin Congdon and Doug Blandy, "Working with Communities and Folk Traditions: Socially Ecological and Culturally Democratic Practice in Art Education," in Doug Boughton and Rachel Mason, eds. *Beyond Multicultural Art Education: International Perspectives* (New York: Waxmann Münster, 1999), 76–77.

11 This seminar was funded by the Getty Education Institute for the Arts and was coordinated by the Art Education Program at Ohio State University. Don Krug was the coordinator and the author was a program planner.

Chapter

6

Art Programs Focusing
on Work and Occupation

Work is often thought of as something that you simply need to do in order to survive. Work can be part of a job or an occupation, or it can be daily activities such as doing the laundry, washing the dishes, or preparing a lunch. The same activity, however, could be considered either work or leisure depending on how it is viewed. For example, if a person hunts because he needs food to eat, it would be called work; if he hunts for pleasure and not because he needs food, the activity would be called leisure. Likewise, planting a garden for food is work, but planting a garden for the joy of producing especially large cabbages, for instance, is a leisure activity.[1]

Try This

Divide a sheet of paper into two columns. List the activities you take part in that you think are work in one column, and those you see as leisure in the other. Share the list with your classmates. Does everyone agree on the list of things placed in each category? If there is disagreement, explain why.

Discussion Point

Read the following quote to the class and ask the students to explain what George Butler meant by it. Ask them if there are other circumstances in which you learn about art and aesthetics where you might miss part of the experience.

"That's the one thing you can't get on your equipment. You can get color and you can get sound, but you can't get smell, and the aroma is the thing. Maybe it's the osmosis of the sap getting into your system, but there is just something about it that makes old-timers who've sugared want to sugar."

—George Butler from Jacksonville, Vermont, talking to Charles Kuralt about the smells in making maple syrup and his inability to capture this on camera.

This chapter deals with art and artistic activities that are related to work and occupation. Because work strongly influences the way we see the world, it is important that teachers address issues related to this necessary part of our lives.

We are all aesthetically influenced by the work environments we are raised in and the kinds of work we do. For instance, if someone grew up with parents who ran a grocery store, she might collect historical postcards of produce. Or if a person paints houses for a living, he might be especially tuned in to the ways in which color changes with the light.

One doesn't have to be personally engaged in a particular occupation to understand its aesthetic dimensions. People who grew up on farms may not think of themselves as farmers, but they probably know about farming. Someone who was raised in a military family may be aware of military bases, uniforms, and how they represent ranks, the experience of moving from state to state, and perhaps country to country. Someone whose parents own or work in a restaurant, a dry-cleaning service, or a bookstore will grow up with an awareness of what that business and workspace is all about. These kinds of understandings can easily affect the way people see the world and influence their aesthetic preferences. It has to do partly with what they pay attention to.

Examples of occupational aesthetics can come from all walks of life. A woman from Astoria, Oregon, who cleans tuna for a living pays attention to the "soft colors" of the fish, "the reds and whites and purples." She understands that the dark meat, which is "crumbly and moist like the earth," becomes cat food. She explained, "I had no idea of the sensuous things I would feel just from cleaning fish."[2] While we may readily identify potters, painters, sculptors, and architects as artists, folklorist Michael Owen Jones points out that we might want to think of many more kinds of workers as artists, as did early anthropologists, such as Franz Boas. For them, early industrial and technological tools were considered art.[3] From this perspective, we can give the name of artist to all kinds of designers, engineers, cooks, beauticians, store window dressers, furniture builders, and many other kinds of workers.[4]

By exploring this perspective of work, teachers can help students open up myriad ways of viewing the world aesthetically. It also opens up the possibility of thinking of one's family members as having an artistic approach to the world.

Even if we hesitate to use such a broad-based definition of artists, we can easily see the influence that various kinds of work have on people who are most readily referred to as artists in our society. Lila Katzen spoke about how she would apportion the time she spent on drawing and on her everyday chores: "I would draw for a half hour, leave it, do a chore, return, draw a half hour, do a chore, begin a sculpture and work forty-five minutes, do a chore."[5] While Katzen switched back and forth between what she considered her art and her work, Beverly Pepper observed that she likes to cook because "you use your hands so much," which is what she does when she makes her sculpture.[6] It is important to remember that our work and art can be closely aligned, and sometimes they are one and the same.

Sometimes artists make statements about aesthetics and work by making some aspect of the work process visible. For example, from 1979 to 1981 Mierle Laderman Ukeles developed and implemented her performance project called "Touch Sanitation," where she listened to New York City sanitation workers talking about being treated as if they were themselves garbage. For the next eleven months, she walked through the city streets, shaking the hands of all the sanitation workers in the city,

Discussion Point

Explain the nature of work and aesthetics presented by the following two cultural perspectives.

"Once a friend of ours was visiting a group of women in a developing country. One morning, the women asked her to come with them to the village well where they filled their pots and jugs with water. As they sat talking, the native women asked their guest how she got her water. 'I have a wonderful room in my house,' she said, 'where there is a metal bowl with metal handles. In between the handles is a spout. Anytime, day or night, I turn the handles and fresh water flows out.' . . . She waited for the women to exclaim, thinking, 'Surely they will be impressed.' But there was only silence. Finally, one of the women looked at the Westerner, proudly dressed in her fine clothes, and said in a quiet voice, 'How lonely for you.'"

—From Annie Cheatham and Mary Clare Powell, *This Way Daybreak Comes: Women's Values and the Future* (Philadelphia: New Society Publisher, 1986), 88.

thanking them for the work they do.[7] In 1993, Regina Frank sewed pearls onto a silk gown for twenty-eight days while sitting in a window of the New Museum in New York City. Each day she made the wages of a seamstress from a different country. The hourly pay ranged from $.20 in Indonesia to $17.10 in Norway, and $6.95 in the United States. By engaging in this act, she wanted viewers to focus, not on the dress she was making, but on the value placed on women textile workers in sweatshops around the world.[8]

This chapter will look at some artworks and art programs that relate to work and occupations. Ways that educators can build their own programs and projects based on these models will be suggested. Like the curricular models in chapter 5, these projects may not all be directly based on folklore, but reflect the aesthetic processes of the everyday that are rooted in communities of work and occupation.

6.1 Fruit stand, Zellwood, Florida, 1987. Photo by Peter Schreyer.

Florida Farmworkers' Documentary Project, "The Last Harvest"

Teachers can look at changing occupational processes in their communities as the foundation for curriculum building. When changes take place, they often result in the loss of jobs and a way of life. While these processes can be difficult, artwork based on these changes can be helpful in making visible the issues that surround the changes. Understanding the past and present is helpful in determining the future. Teachers can involve students in art projects that engage them in this dialogue. "The Last Harvest" documentary project is a good example of how this kind of participation can work.

In the summer of 1997, twenty-five hundred central Florida farmworkers—Mexican Americans, Appalachian Whites, Haitians, Puerto Ricans, Guatemalans, and African-Americans—were told

they would be out of a job in less than a year. Florida's legislature purchased the farms they had worked on for forty to fifty years in an effort to restore the ecological balance to Lake Apopka, since repeated fertilizing had polluted the area.

The Farmworkers' Association of Florida approached several local organizations for help in documenting their occupational and cultural history before it was lost. While many organizations eventually participated in the resulting documentary project, Crealde School of Art, in Winter Park, immediately began working with young adults from farming families to teach them photography, so that they could capture images of their economic, social, and cultural contributions to the local area.[9] Numerous photographs and text panels came from this effort.

Folklorists, photographers, teachers, historians, colleges, and funding organizations all worked with the Farmworkers' Association of Florida to gather the necessary information, both verbally and visually.

The resulting show, "The Last Harvest: A History and Tribute to the Life and Work of the Farmworkers on Lake Apopka," traveled around Florida cities, and now tours the Southeast. A panel of participants discussed their experiences and their occupational culture with audiences at many of the Florida exhibition sites. When the exhibition is finished traveling, all field notes and photographs will be archived for public access.

While a way of life was lost forever, the history of the farmworkers in Apopka will not disappear. In the midst of one of the most difficult periods in these

Looking for a Better Life

"I came to the United States in 1980 looking for a better life. I came by boat with twenty-three other people. It took eleven days to get here because it was so stormy. We carried big barrels of drinking water to the boat to survive. We learned to use the water wisely. When I got here I was put in jail for two days. I have seven children in Haiti, but it's very hard to bring them here. Still, life is better in the United States. If you're not lazy, you can find work."

—Louis Nicisse, a Haitian farmworker who lost his job due to the closing of the farms at Lake Apopka; from a text panel from the exhibition "The Last Harvest"

Try This

Talk to new immigrants in your community and find out what kinds of occupations are available to them. Explain why these jobs are available and others are not. Make a visual description of what you learned.

6.2 Grading Carrots, Zellwin Packing House, Apopka, Florida, 1998, from the exhibition, "The Last Harvest." Photo by Felipe Gonzalez, courtesy of Crealde School of Art, Winter Park, Florida.

families' lives, they knew that their history was important, and they took the time to make sure it would be remembered. Artists, teachers, and students with cameras helped make this remembrance possible.

Classroom Connections: Changing Jobs, Changing Communities

Art educators might use "The Last Harvest" as a model for projects in their own communities, posing the following kinds of questions to students:

• Is there an occupational community in your area that is being phased out? If so, who works in this occupation?
• How will the change affect your community?
• What might you want future generations to know about the cultural history of this occupation?

Teachers might then ask students how they might use art to document and interpret the changes before and after they take place. Students would need to identify individuals and organizations to help with the project, making a visual plan that explains their project idea. This could take the form of charts, timelines, an artist book, collages, a website, or a written dialogue with photos of participants. The idea might then be presented to a class or community group, with students completing the project with the community partnerships they have made.

Engaging students in a process such as "The Last Harvest" teaches them about being good citizens, and empowers them to realize that they have a voice in preserving occupational traditions. Additionally, a process such as this one demonstrates to students various connections between art and work. These connections are often not clearly delineated, and sometimes the aesthetic component involved

can make art and work seem much like the same thing.

While it may be easy to see that blue-collar work, especially that which is related to the landscape, can have an aesthetic dimension, it may be more difficult to see that white-collar work also has an aesthetic component.

The University of Washington's Orthodontic Sculpture

Many professionals' jobs demand that they have an aesthetic sensibility in order to do the work well. Teachers can make this aspect of work visible to their students, thereby enabling them to understand the importance of good art education.

Orthodontists need to know how to solve problems creatively with good design and technical skill in order to do their job successfully. At the University of Washington, Professor Stanton Hall taught metal sculpting to his orthodontic students as a way of helping them learn. He remarked that this approach "not only accomplished the minimal task of familiarizing the student with the materials, but also exercised their creative and aesthetic appreciation." The class culminated in an exhibition and an award presentation.[10]

Many students who learned this sculptural approach from Professor Hall continue to make metal sculptures even though they've graduated and are now putting braces on their own patients. Their sculptures include tree ornaments or self-standing sculptural pieces, both representational and abstract. While these sculptural pieces can clearly be seen as artwork, the orthodontists who make them are also apt to see the work they do on a patient's braces as artwork. Teachers can make these connections visible as they engage students in a variety of questions about occupations and aesthetics.

Classroom Connections: Researching
Local Work Aesthetics

Teachers might work with students using this orthodontic example as a model. Many students have
undergone orthodontic work and might be able to
call their orthodontists to ask questions about how
they view their work aesthetically. An interview with
a local orthodontist might include questions about
design, problem solving, technical skills, and aesthetic considerations. Students might also ask orthodontists about educational practices such as those
used in the University of Washington class, and how
orthodontists see themselves in relation to the art
world.

Teachers and students might brainstorm about
other kinds of occupational groups in their community who might engage in similar artistic activities.
Students might list activities in which artists engage
(such as designing, welding, or building), then interview members from other occupational groups to
see if they participate in any of the same activities.
Students might take photographs or draw pictures,
correlating the activities they feel are similar. Students might explore the work of engineers, car sales-
people, tree trimmers, attorneys, or physicians. When
engaging in this activity, students should compare
the skills and inquiry practices of these occupational
groups with a wide range of artists, including
graphic designers, fabric artists, landscape designers,
and performance artists.

It may be useful to lead students in studying the
culture of another group that has been documented
by an anthropologist. Suggested groups of people
might be nineteenth-century Northwest Coast Native
Americans, Australian Aborigines, or Africans living
on the Ivory Coast today. Students might compare
and contrast the ways occupational groups in these
cultures are described by anthropologists and the

Discussion Point

One could assume that orthodontists
would want their children to have
straight teeth and a healthy bite, and
if they needed it, would recommend
braces. Why then would a Tidewater,
North Carolina, resident say this about
taxidermy: "There is . . . [a] common
taboo in interior decorations: it is considered the height of bad taste to display
things from the wild unless they have
been fundamentally transformed. No
one displays stuffed ducks or fish, even
though the area is known for hunting
and fishing and some guides practice
taxidermy for the tourists. Taxidermy is
deemed a 'foreign' habit that violates a
basic local premise of sporting: fish and
game are for eating."

–Quoted in John Forrest's *Lord I'm*
Coming Home: *Everyday Aesthetics in*
Tidewater North Carolina (Ithaca: Cornell
University Press, 1988), 61–62.

Try This

Talk to family members or neighbors
who work outside the home and ask
them to think of themselves as artists in
their positions. See if they can describe
something they do from an aesthetic
viewpoint. Write about one of these
people, describing them as an artist.

ways we think about these occupational groups and their identities as artists in the United States today. Is there a difference, and why or why not? Could folklorist Michael Owen Jones be right with his idea that we neglect to see as art much of the work that is done in our culture?

Art teachers building curriculum around this model might work with teachers in other disciplines such as social studies, health, or science. These teachers' expertise is often very helpful, and they may be able to discuss many of the content issues in their own classrooms, which would enrich the students' overall experience.

African-American Sea Grass Basketry

African-Americans, primarily women, on the eastern seaboard north of Charleston, South Carolina have been practicing the art of coiled sea grass basketry without interruption, for more than three hundred years. This may be the oldest artistic activity of African origin in the United States. Oftentimes, men and children get involved in the process, and "an aesthetic community centered around basket making" is formed.[11] These baskets have been sold to tourists visiting Charleston for more than a century. Roadside stands for selling the baskets can be found on Highway 17 from Charleston to Mt. Pleasant. Tourists purchase them as regional folk art and mementos of their visit. Museums around the country also collect these baskets.

With increased development in the Southeast, the sea grass used to make the baskets has become scarce. And if sea grasses still exist in the area, resorts and subdivisions, designed to accommodate the needs of the tourists and new arrivals to the area, have cut off access to areas where these grasses grow. New development has also crowded out the spots where roadside stands used to be.

These changes force basket makers and their family members to travel far from home to gather grasses in order to continue their businesses. This crisis was documented as early as 1971. As a result, the artists organized and requested help from local government officials, historians, folklorists, museum curators, and other concerned citizens. Some changes have been made to secure areas where the sea grasses will remain available to basket makers, and roadside stands appear to be surviving on Highway 17. Bullrush is blended with the sea grasses to make it stretch, giving new color and dimension to the tradition, and communities of basket makers often work together to gather the grasses from local areas. Still, many weavers continue to travel to North Florida to gather sea grass, some of which, they say, is longer and stronger than the grasses they are able to get locally.

6.3 *Margaret Garrison, sea grass basket maker. Photo courtesy of the Florida Folklife Program, Division of Historical Resources.*

Like most folk arts, sea grass basket making is both traditional and dynamic. It maintains its roots, but changes with the times. Along with these changes and the long-lasting traditions come proverbs, tales, jokes, and legends. Different shapes, styles, and uses for the baskets are continually being found, and occupational lifestyles are generally maintained.

These sea grass baskets and their makers present art teachers with a good opportunity to teach students how occupations can directly relate to the environment. When the environment changes, materials and ways of selling sometimes have to change as well. Teachers can lead students in debates about what is important to save in an environment, who should make these decisions, and what the consequences of change might be. Discussions like these can lead students into other kinds of discussion about what we should value and how we should go about preserving it.

Classroom Connections: Learning about Basketry Traditions

Teachers might encourage students to research more about basketry traditions as an occupation. Students could compare and contrast how the African-American basketry traditions in South Carolina relate to basketry traditions in other parts of the country, such as those of Native American basket makers working in the Appalachian or Ozark regions.

Teachers and students might explore how a group's basketry traditions relate to the environment in which its members live. Both the materials and functions of the baskets can be researched. Students can find out who buys the baskets and why. Are they used, or are they enjoyed solely as decorative items? Issues related to how the baskets have changed over time could be studied and a timeline of these

Discussion Point

Discuss what Robert Davidson, a Haida artist from the Northwest Coast Native American culture, means by the following statement:

"The only way tradition can be carried on is to keep inventing new things."

Does this statement sound like a paradox to you? What does he mean? How does this apply to a traditional artistic practice in your community?

—Quote from William Severini Kowinski, "Giving New Life to Haida Art and the Culture It Expresses," *Smithsonian* 25, no. 10 (January 1995): 38-47.

Discussion Point

In Toni Morrison's novel *Beloved* (New York: Knopf, 1987) the character named Sethe would often fold laundry and knead dough to calm her sorrow. Can you explain this behavior? Do you ever do work to make yourself feel better when you are sad? What do aesthetics have to do with this activity, if anything at all? Do artists create when they are sad or happy? Does it make a difference? How?

changes, and why they have taken place, made. Historical drawings and photographs might be added to the timeline. Basket makers could be interviewed and asked about how they have experienced change related to their basketry and what caused that change.

Using the model of the South Carolina basket makers, students could identify materials they have in their environment and make a container that relates to their cultural heritage. After the containers have been made, teachers might ask students the following questions:

- Who might purchase your basket if you were to make the basket your livelihood?
- How can you market them? How might you involve family members in the process?
- Are your materials plentiful?
- What might make the supply dwindle?
- Who might you contact to make sure you have the necessary supply of materials you need?

This exercise can be a valuable one for students because it helps them work through issues related to their own cultural heritage, and it encourages them to think about how they might use various materials from their own environment. It may help them understand that sometimes progress has a downside, and that decisions that are made to improve an area from one person's perspective might not be an improvement based on another's viewpoint. Students might also be able to see that when change takes place and it negatively affects one's work, decisions can be made that might improve the artistic process. In other words, sometimes change that is viewed negatively presents an artist with an opportunity to explore new ways of creating traditional products.

Crop Art by Stan Herd

Stan Herd's art grew out of his farming experience. He was raised in Kansas on a 160-acre farm with cattle, horses, and wheat. The farm was started by his grandfather, who broke ground in 1916. As Stan Herd rode the family tractor and worked with his father, he wondered what people saw when they were looking down at his farm from the sky.

In 1969, encouraged by his family, Herd left the farm to study art at Wichita State University. Then, in the 1970s, he saw a television documentary on the unexplained Nazca lines in the Peru desert. These large-scale, ancient line drawings in the earth could only be seen from the air. He also became aware of the artist Christo, who made the twenty-four-mile *Running Fence* across a California hillside. His interest was stirred by these notable experiences, and he began to think about how he might make art that would be based on his own experiences; that's when the idea for crop art came to him.[12] He started planting various colorful crops in such a way that, seen from the air, they depicted images much like a painting. Some works are so large and on such flat terrain that they can only be seen from the air, while others can be viewed from a hillside, roadway, or window from an upper floor of a skyscraper.

One of his best-known pieces, *Sunflower Still Life,* which occupied twenty acres of land, reminds us of one of van Gogh's sunflower paintings. It is also reflective of how beautiful a well-grown field of crops can look. This one included a variety of alfalfa, soybeans, and sunflowers. Herd helps us view the landscape in a way that we may have forgotten how to do as we have removed ourselves further and further from the land.

Herd likes to work in collaboration, usually with local residents, but students from other areas also come to plant and harvest his crops. In New York, he worked with homeless people and they harvested crops to help feed themselves and others. The work, then, is understood and appreciated in a cyclical manner, much like the aesthetics of everyday farming.

Teachers can use Stan Herd's art to demonstrate how individuals can make art based on their occupational expertise. This example might provide a model for students to think about how people from various occupational groups could use what they know and turn it into a new kind of art form. Sometimes seeing things from another perspective makes a big difference. Sometimes a change in scale can turn something into art. An example of this is the work of Claes Oldenburg and Coosje van Bruggen, who take everyday objects like clothespins or hamburgers and recreate the form in architectural size. In addition to changing scale, sometimes placing an ordinary object in a new context makes something seem more like an artwork, as Marcel Duchamp exemplified with his readymades.

Classroom Connections: Designing with Plant Life
In some areas it might be easy to identify students who have lived on a farm or spent significant amounts of time on a farm. If you work in an urban area and none of the students have farming experience, you might consider bringing a farmer into the classroom to talk about Stan Herd's work from a farming perspective. You might then invite an artist to talk about the same work. Ask students to explain how each guest speaker's approach to the same work varies. An analysis could also be done on each visitor's use of language. The following questions could be asked of students:

- Who appears to know more about the aesthetics of Stan Herd's work, the farmer or the artist?
- Based on what you know about art, and what the

Discuss the gender difference in farm aesthetics using the following quote from Jane Smiley's book *A Thousand Acres:*

"But mostly, farm women are proud of the fact that they can keep the house looking as though the farm stays outside, that the curtains are white and sparkling and starched, that the carpet is clean and the windowsills dusted and the furniture in good shape, or at least neatly slipcovered (by the wife). Just as the farmers cast measuring glances at each other's buildings, judging states of repair and ages of paint jobs, their wives never fail to give the house a close inspection for dustballs, cobwebs, dirty windows. And just as farmers love new, more efficient equipment, farmwives are real connoisseurs of household appliances: whole-house vacuum cleaners mounted in the walls, microwave ovens and crock-pots, chest freezers, through-the-door icemakers on refrigerators, heavy duty washers and dryers, pot-scrubbing dishwashers and electric deep fat fryers."

Do you think this quote accurately portrays farm women today? What would a farm family in your community say about this apparent difference between men and women?

—Quote from Jane Smiley, *A Thousand Acres* (New York: Knopf, 1991), 120.

Discussion Point

The following quote is from Ana Castello's novel, *So Far from God*. Discuss the character in terms of people students know who take on characteristics of their work.

"But over seven generations of sheepherding had invariably gotten into Casey's blood, so that even though nobody would ever admit it, and it was hard to actually prove—since Casey was such a soft-spoken man to begin with—Fe was certain that her fiancé had somehow acquired the odd affliction of bleating.

"It was like this: Sometimes he'd be working in his office at night and if she was around . . . and thought that maybe he'd like a cup of osha, knowing how much he suffered from indigestion, just outside his door she'd hear a soft but distinct ba-aaa sound. Maybe it's his heartburn, she'd say to herself, or maybe he's just tired, as if bleating were the natural sound men made when yawning, or burping for that matter.

"But eventually, she began to notice him doing this on the street, in actual broad daylight, in public, although not quite in front of her, since he was always maybe two or three feet ahead of her whenever it would happen, in the Broadway picking out new underwear, let's say, when out of modesty, Fe was intentionally staying behind a bit. She was sure she heard a bleat. She'd look around quickly to see if anyone else had heard it too. But as it happened, nobody else was ever near enough to hear it, if, in fact, that was what it was.

"After a few months, there was no doubt that her fiancé had this inbred peculiarity that couldn't be helped, as I said, after three hundred years of sheepbreeding and a long line of ancestors spending lifetimes of long, cold winters tending their herds."

—Quote from Ana Castello, *So Far from God* (New York: W. W. Norton & Company, 1993), 175.

visitors taught you, explain the "art" part of Stan Herd's work.

- If Stan Herd had not been raised on a farm, do you think he would have been able to do this kind of art? Why or why not?

After having an in-depth discussion about Herd's work, you might ask students to do the following art project. On a piece of paper, they design a work of crop art and explain the kinds of plants they need to grow for it to be successful. A science teacher might be helpful in answering questions about the kinds of crops that can be grown together, the colors of each plant during specific times of the year, and the horizontal scale of each. Students can then talk about what might be done with the artwork when it is harvested and whether or not they would consider that part of the effort to be "art."

Teachers might ask students to collaboratively grow a small work of crop art either on school grounds or in the community. Students could then relate to another class or community group what they had to learn in order to accomplish the project. They could explain what kinds of occupational groups they contacted to do the work, and describe which parts of the project they believe to be "artwork." Be aware of the fact that within the group, there may be diverse perspectives on what constitutes art.

Students might be asked to research other contemporary artists who use the earth as a canvas for their art, working individually or in groups to do presentations on these artists. In concluding this project, teachers might want to explore with students what occupational groups use the same skills as the artists presented, and if these workers can also be considered artists. Students should be prepared to defend their answers.

These crop-related activities can assist students in seeing artistic potential in the ways we manipulate the earth. This exploration also helps to teach students to see objects and the environment from perspectives and viewpoints different from the norm. Teachers can explain that how we see things can change their meanings and our way of thinking about them.

Everyone who works manipulates some kind of materials. Because artists also work with materials, and these materials increasingly are becoming more varied, teachers can help students explore new creative possibilities. Workers can become artists and artists can gather inspiration from studying various occupational groups. Teachers can help students make these connections by studying work activities, occupational aesthetics, and our relationship to varying kinds of materials.

Notes

1 This distinction between work and leisure is made by Michael Owen Jones in "A Feeling for Form," in Nikolai Burlakoff and Carl Lindahl, eds. *Folklore on Two Continents: Essays in Honor of Linda Degh* (Bloomington, IN: Trickster Press, 1980), 260–69.

2 Ibid., 261.

3 Ibid., 260.

4 For a more complete discussion of this broadened perspective, see Kristin G. Congdon, "Occupational Art and Occupational Influences on Aesthetic Preferences: A Democratic Perspective," in *Art in a Democracy,* Doug Blandy and Kristin G. Congdon (New York: Teachers College Press, 1987), 110–23. Also related is Michael Owen Jones's chapter "Making Work Art and Artwork: The Aesthetic Impulse in Organizations and Education" in the same anthology, pages 124–37.

5 See Eleanor Monro, *Originals: American Women Artists* (New York: Simon and Schuster, 1979), 228–29.

6 Ibid., 347.

7 For information on this performance piece and other works by Ukeles in the New York Sanitation Department, see Judith Stein "Collaboration," in Norma Broude and Mary D. Garrand, eds. *The Power of Feminist Art* (New York: Harry N. Abrams, 1994), 226-45, and Patricia C. Phillips, "Public Art: Waste Not," *Art in America* (February 1989): 47, 49, and 51.

8 For a more complete description of this project see "Where Women Sew a Lot but Reap a Little," *Parade Magazine* (November 7, 1993): 16.

9 While Crealde School of Art took a leadership role in this documentation project, many other groups played instrumental roles as well. Included are the Farmworkers' Association of Florida, the Florida Folklore Society, Seminole Community College, and the Florida Humanities Council.

10 Personal communication, August 5, 1985.

11 See Gerald L. Davis, "Afro-American Coil Basketry in Charleston County, South Carolina: Affective Characteristics of an Artistic Craft in a Social Context," in Don Yoder, ed. *American Folklife* (Austin: University of Texas Press, 1976), 151–84. For other information on these basket makers, see the article by Dale Rosengarten, "Lowcountry Basketry: Folk Arts in the Marketplace," *Southern Folklore* 49, no. 3 (1992): 240–55, and Mary Twining "Harvesting and Heritage: A Comparison of Afro-American and African Basketry," in *Afro-American Folk Arts and Crafts,* William Ferris, ed. (Boston: G. K. Hall & Co., 1983), 258–71.

12 Jim Robbins, "A Tractor Instead of a Brush; Seeds Instead of Paint," *Smithsonian* 25, no. 4 (July 1994): 70–77. See also Steven Durland, "Duchess County: 'Farm Again': Crop Art," *High Performance #68*, 17, no. 4 (Winter 1994): 44–45 and Stan Herd, *Crop Art and Other Earthworks* (New York: H. N. Abrams, 1994).

Art Programs Focusing on Recreation

Folklorists include recreational groups in their definition of folk groups. In other words, when a group of people routinely gather for the purposes of enjoying a leisure activity, they form a cultural group with a particular way of enjoying and speaking about what it is they do.

His Love of Lowriders

"For me, cars were not just art, they were everything. . . . Wherever I found myself, kids bought them, talked them, drew them, and dreamed them—hopped them up and dropped them down— cruised them on the drag and dragged them on the highway, and I did too."

—From Dave Hickey, *Air Guitar: Essays on Art and Democracy* (Los Angeles: Art Issues, 1997), 61.

"I would define a lowrider as something that is low, something that has custom paint, something that has a lot of shiny chrome, whether it be gold or chrome. And some type of wire wheels. And definitely something with hydraulics. That, to me, would be a lowrider. And upholstery. The upholstery has to have some kind of custom twist to it."

—Ernie Rulas, quoted in *Arte y Estilo: The Lowriding Tradition* by Denise Sandoval and Patrick A. Polk (Los Angeles: Peterson Automotive Museum, 2000), 17.

For example, people who engage in automobile lowriding traditions have a language developed specifically to explain their artistic process and its aesthetic. Creating a lowrider is often a family affair, which helps establish an identity for the participants and aids in the development of a sense of community, most often centered in Mexican-American neighborhoods. In recreating automobiles, the cars are recontextualized. Instead of going for speed, they become "slow and low," thereby reversing the aesthetic of the mainstream culture, negating more dominant models and values, such as speed.[1] In this way, Mexican-American communities define themselves as separate and apart from other communities. They build on this identity with ritualized artistic processes that define and redefine who they are.

People gather around all kinds of recreational activities, all of which have aesthetic dimensions. Golfers know about curves on the golf course and directions of the blowing wind. They appreciate a well-made club, and often dress in such a distinctive way that makes nongolfers chuckle. Gardeners are ubiquitous all over the United States, and good ones know how to succeed in growing colorful flowers, flavorful tomatoes, or herbs. They learn from friends and trial-and-error. They go to orchid shows, attend workshops about cooking with herbs, or learn about the most effective fertilizers for their environmental conditions and plants. Some people create yard art to distinguish their lawns from the neighbors' while communicating their own value-based aesthetics. For example, in the South some African-Americans still sweep their yards, viewing weeds or grass as hindrances to daily chores done in the yard, while residents in some suburban areas might choose to carefully trim trees into unnatural formations.[2]

Parks in many cities now have public art pieces that integrate play and aesthetics with learning experiences. One example is the Kwanzaa Playground in Columbus, Ohio, created by Shirley Bowen, her young son, and seven other artists of African descent. Children come to play in this playground, but that's not all—the design of the space and the playground equipment encourages "lessons for living" based on Kwanzaa's seven principles: unity, self-determination, collective work and responsibility, cooperative economics, purpose, creativity, and faith.[3]

There may be parks in your community that exist to teach particular lessons. For example, some parks have historical buildings that have been renovated. The purpose of these parks is to teach visitors about local history. Other parks are set up to explore the plant life in them, while others focus on the birds or animals that inhabit the space. In each case, the space has been changed in some artistic manner to encourage a learning experience.

There are many other ways that recreational experiences incorporate aesthetic decisions. Artistic elements may be found in game boards, sports equipment, body adornment and fashion, party favors, cooking, holiday decorations, and home altars. People collect objects such as refrigerator magnets, snow domes, costume jewelry, and salt and pepper shakers. When we have leisure time, we often opt to use it by doing something we are drawn to simply for the pleasure it gives us. Usually, there are aesthetic dimensions to the activities we enjoy. Many leisure activities revolve around rites of passage and celebrations such as birthday parties, parades, or other holiday events. Teachers can encourage students to identify celebrations they participate in, and the artistic activities that are related to each one. These celebrations might be categorized into topics such as clothing, decorations, and food-related activities.

This chapter will look at some artworks and programs that relate to recreational activities. Ways that educators can build on these models will be suggested. Folkloric elements are associated with each of these activities because they involve processes practiced by cultural groups. Even so, some of the results may be so innovative, popular, or extreme that they move out of the realm considered traditional by most folklorists.

7.1 *Unidentified Florida woman with cake. Photo courtesy of the Florida Folklife Programs, Division of Historical Resources.*

Try This

Ask your students to bring in as many game boards as they can. Display them around the classroom. Compare and contrast their designs. Design a new game board with an appealing design, then invent a game to go with it.

Try This

Many young students like to dress up at Halloween or during other times of the year for parties, parades or Carnivals, theatrical events, or holidays. Discuss this activity and why people do it. Imagine what kind of role you might like to take on next. Get a picture of yourself from your home and paint and decorate it so that you can become that person. Discuss why you chose that image. Place the finished piece in a context that will spark discussion about your artwork.

7.2 Key West, Florida, festival. Photo by Bud Lee.

Chapter 7

Northwest Ohio's "Art of Fishing" Exhibition

In the Spring of 1987, Doug Blandy and Kristin Congdon coordinated an exhibition in Bowling Green State University's Art Gallery focusing on local fishing aesthetics. Experts in various fishing traditions such as fly tying, rod wrapping, and taxidermy were located and invited to participate. These experts curated sections of the gallery, and several of them acted as fishers-in-residence on the opening day. Old postcards and family snapshots were displayed, along with carved fishing lures, and other specialized fishing gear. Fish was fried using local recipes, coolers were packed as if ready for a fishing trip, and old fishing films were shown. Storytelling, both formally arranged and impromptu, took place everywhere.

Students from local schools and community centers visited the exhibition, and when they could not, Congdon and Blandy showed slides of the exhibit with special emphasis on the old postcards that portrayed outrageous fishing experiences. These images were used to encourage an exchange of exaggerated fish tales. Students were then given blank postcards and asked to draw their own fish story on the front. On the back they wrote about the experience and addressed the card to a friend or relative. Images included extraordinarily large fish in boats, in trucks, on top of cars, and in the water. In the postcards, students showed themselves being eaten by large fish, and, in various ways, overwhelmed by them. Students also drew exceptionally large fish being cooked and placed them in many other kinds of humorous situations. Many of the fish on these postcards were smart, technologically advanced, and ready for any kind of challenge. This activity has been recreated in other schools since the exhibition closed.[4]

Discussion Point

An evaluation form left by the Bowling Green State University "Art of Fishing" exhibition asked this question: "Are you an artist?" One answer given was this: "Yes, because I fish." Explain what was meant by this interpretation of the question. Is this a reasonable response? Why or why not?

Discussion Point

Read this quote from *Memoirs of a Geisha* by Arthur Golden (New York: Alfred A. Knopf, 1987), 428. It is a statement made by the main character in the novel who is telling her story:

"I've lived my life again just by telling it to you."

Explain what she means and relate it to storytelling activities such as telling a fish tale.

7.3 *Fishing postcard by Jerry Drosky, grade five, Sterling Park Elementary School, Casselberry, Florida. Teacher: Karen Branen.*

Classroom Connections: The Art of Fishing in Your Community

Lakes, rivers, and oceans help define communities all over the world. Many of these bodies of water invite fishing practices. Consider talking to students about local fishing traditions, and asking them the following questions:

- Who fishes in our community?
- Why do they fish? What makes for a good fishing trip?
- What do fishers take with them on a fishing trip?
- How do they make or personalize these objects?

Ask students to describe the best fishing trip they have ever been on. After describing it, ask students to exaggerate it to extremes in a picture of the trip on a postcard. On the reverse side of the card students can tell the story, address the postcard to a friend or relative, and send it.

Consider asking students to invent a new kind of fishing lure to catch the ultimate fish. The lure can be created in both two-dimensional and three-dimensional form. To extend the lesson further, students can describe or draw a picture of the fish the lure is designed to catch. Create an exhibition of the lures and drawings in a public space. Text panels can describe the fish that would be caught. Ask students to think about the audience and purpose of the exhibit. The design can focus on an exhibition space aimed at selling the newly designed lures, or an art space with text panels created to convince art critics that the lures are great works of art. Students could then discuss how the approach, language, and end result would differ.

The fishing exhibition can be used as a model for other kinds of exhibitions that might reflect the community. These exhibitions might center on recreational activities such as bicycling, skateboarding, roller-blading, hiking, camping, golfing, equestrian events, boating, tractor-pulls, dog shows and other animal shows such as those that might be found at a country fair, and other traditions such as quilting, jam making, or flower competitions. Students might brainstorm ways they would make artistic items and their related traditions understandable to a gallery visitor.

Manuel Vega and Cuban Birdcages and Kites

Along with thousands of other Cubans, Manuel Vega came to Miami to live during the Cuban Revolution of 1959. In his small hometown of San Antonio de las Vueltas he was known as an expert in making festival objects that he created for the annual cele- brations of the town's patron saint. He has made *farolas* (decorative lanterns carried by carnival partic- ipants), floats, and costumes, and he is also known for his woodworking expertise. In the past he has made cabinets, guitars, and boats.

In Miami, Vega continues the Cuban traditions of making birdcages for songbirds that, in Cuba, would be captured and cared for on patios. His elaborate birdcages are now made for friends or are sold to pet stores. Many are carefully constructed architec- tural works with intricate details and fanciful win- dows and doors. Made from metal and various kinds of wood, some of these sculpture-like artworks are purchased by collectors simply to adorn houses.

It is also a Cuban tradition to make six-sided kites that are flown by children in Cuba and in Florida's Cuban communities of Ybor City and Key West. Some of the kites resemble Chinese kites, since so many Chinese immigrated to Cuba and shared their kite-making traditions there. Because Manuel Vega makes such wonderful birdcages and kites, he won the prestigious Florida Folk Heritage Award in 1998.[5]

Classroom Connections: Diversity in Kites and Kite Making

Teachers might ask their students to study kite-mak- ing traditions from various countries. Differences in designs can be discussed in the classroom as students talk about the ways they relate to their own kite experiences. A science teacher or knowledgeable

7.4 Birdcage by Manuel Vega. Photo courtesy of the Historical Museum of Southern Florida, Miami, Florida.

A Beautiful Sight

"The reason I like flying kites, you're always looking up. You're not looking down like you do when you're playing golf or some of the other things. You're looking up at that pretty blue sky. It is a beautiful sight."

—Ansel Tony, an eighty-nine-year-old kite-maker from Farmland, Indiana, in Charles Kuralt, *On the Road* (New York: G. P. Putman's Sons, 1985), 227.

Try This

Ask your students to design a community park that would teach an important lesson. This can be done either individually or as a group. For instance, ask students how they might design a community park to teach local history. (Red Grooms' *Tennessee Fox Trot Carousel* is an example. The artist designed the carousel so that people could "ride" on a tour bus of an important Tennessee country singer or on Davy Crockett's horse.)

community scientist, perhaps an aerospace engineer, can be invited to talk about the dynamics of kite flying. Students could select a design and decorate it with symbols from their own community. On a windy day, students will be able to fly their kites, making a visual display of their artworks.

Teachers might ask students what other kinds of recreational objects they play with that are similar to kites. Various kinds of paper airplanes, for example, might be explored. Creating snow or sand sculptures might also be topics of discussion, depending on the location of one's community.

An art unit might also be built around birdcages. Students could choose a kind of bird that would make an appropriate pet, study the bird, and write an essay from the bird's perspective on what kind of birdcage it would like to live in. Students could either draw a design for the birdcage or actually create it. Teachers might ask students to write another essay from the bird's perspective on what was accomplished according to the planned expectations, and what didn't come out quite right. Students might talk to someone who has built a house and then lived in it. Teachers might ask them to describe the common problems and restrictions that the home-builder and the student (as the bird) had with their experiences. The class can compare the experience of the student-as-bird and the homebuilder.

A good lesson can also focus on spaces in people's homes, like patios, family rooms, and porches. Students identify the spaces where their families gather to talk and share quality time and describe what kinds of objects make that space special.

Another lesson might focus on Manuel Vega as an example of an artist who creates objects for local festivals. Students might look into their community traditions to identify people who take this role in their local festivals. They might compare how the objects are made, whether they are kept or remade each year, and how the objects and the maker are valued in their respective communities.

Students can also invent a celebration they think would be fun for their community. They could explore what it would look like, who would participate, what experiences would take place and what kinds of artistic skills would be needed. Sharing these ideas with the rest of the class encourages imaginative thinking as it helps students formulate ideas about their own community identity.

John Ahearn and Rigoberto Torres and Community Sculptures

John Ahearn and Rigoberto Torres collaborate on artworks that are grounded in the everyday experience of everyday people. While Torres now lives in Florida, he is best known for the work he did with Ahearn in the Bronx when he lived there. They made life-sized casts of neighborhood people engaging in activities such as roller-blading, double-dutch jump-rope, listening to boom boxes, and simply appearing in everyday poses. For fifteen years they worked in a storefront and on the streets. The castings were public events, engaging the local community and encouraging enthusiastic participation. Many of the casts are displayed in the homes of those who have been cast, and others travel to galleries and museums worldwide. Some are attached to buildings in the Bronx and may be seen by the public.[6]

The process of making these casts is seen as a community-building process. It is important that students recognize the ways in which artists are sometimes able to engage groups of people in creative processes so that they can envision projects that might be collaborative, public, and team building.

Teachers might consider asking their students to list some of the recreational activities performed by everyday people in their community, and then ask the following questions:

- If you were going to be cast by John Ahearn and Rigoberto Torres, how would you like to be portrayed?
- Think about whether you would want to be in a group scene or portrayed individually.
- Where would you want your cast to be displayed?
- Why would you choose this context?

Lead students in a discussion on what the selected positions say about the individuals involved and the group as a whole. Steer the dialogue to make issues of class, gender, and ethnicity visible as they relate to leisure activities. Students could talk about activities that are done in small groups and those that thrive with large audiences.

Students might research ways that casts can safely be made of the face. They could work with a partner and make each other's face cast. Students might be asked to describe what they have learned, both about the act of casting and being cast, and also about the positioning of the face and what it says about the artwork and the individual. Based on this experience, students might describe how much more difficult it would be to do the kinds of casting that Ahearn and Torres do. Teachers might ask students how they would create arms, mouths, eyes, and full-body casts.

An older group of students could "adopt" a younger group of students. One-on-one interviews with each younger student identifies a favorite leisure time activity. Portraits of the adopted stu-

Discussion Point

Is surfing an art or something else? Read the following quote and discuss whether the writer is engaged in art criticism:

"To some, the riding of waves is a religion; to others it's a sport—good healthy exercise and, they claim, nothing more. Some have said it's an ephemeral transient art form. If surfing is an art, perhaps it is a martial art, but in the spirit of aikido, the Art of Peace, using the opponent's own force to overcome.

"This is the action of a man carving a surfboard on a wave: The wave tightens into a fist of power, the surfer moves into the barrel to greet it. The muscle relaxes, the fist opens and pulls back, the surfer slams off the wide-open face of the wave laying the shoreward rail of his board into a clean arc of beatific contempt. Bit much, eh? Well, from the perspective of the artist surfer, it's just a very beautiful thing."

—Drew Kampion, *Stoked: A History of Surf Culture* (Santa Monica: General Publishing Group, 1997), 149.

dent could be created in media other than plaster casting. These might be life-size paintings that are cut out and displayed somewhere in the school building. Digital photo images could be made and manipulated to show students engaged in some of their favorite activities. The artworks could also be made into a PowerPoint presentation that is run on a "loop" and placed on view for the entire school to enjoy.

Surfers and Surfing Practices

In the 1940s and '50s, youth on the East and West Coasts of the United States discovered surfing. Specialty boards like the Hollow Board, the Hot Curl Board, Pig Boards, and Hobies were created. Numerous beach movies were filmed, many starring Frankie Avalon and Annette Funicello. Recording artists like the Beach Boys and Dick Dale got everyone excited about "catching a wave." A serious

7.5 Palm Beach, Florida, surfers. Photo by Bud Lee.

Chapter 7

surfer (who was usually male) had to have a certain look: a deep tan, sun-bleached long hair, and casual clothes that included sandals, T-shirts, and flowered shirts. Surfboards, surf music, and surf fashion has changed, but it remains a popular sport with an aesthetic clearly related to the thrill of riding the surf. Today the sport is more diverse in gender, age, and ethnicity. Surfing is so popular and pervasive that collectors have created a hot market for surfing memorabilia, and the California Surf Museum recently opened up in Oceanside, California, dedicated to "the artifacts and achievements of the boys and girls of endless summer."[7]

Classroom Connections: Community Sports and Their Aesthetics

Teachers might ask students to list the sports that are popular in their communities. Ask them to answer the following questions about the sports activities on their lists:

- Are they related in any way to the environment?
- Can they be done in some places and not others?
- Does the environment have anything to do with the aesthetic enjoyment of the sport?
- What kinds of objects are created for use in the sport?
- Are any of them handmade? Describe the language and clothing that are central to the sporting activity.

Students might create logos for the sport and the uniforms that go with it, with the logos then presented to the class and students guessing what kinds of activities they symbolize. Ask students to identify other kinds of artistic creations (music, songs, cheers, mascots, tailgate parties, etc.) that occur because of the sport.

Discussion Point

Folklorist Michael Owen Jones observed that one of the most difficult tasks in studying a folk group's aesthetics is how to understand it if an individual doesn't verbalize about it. Some critics even say that without verbalizing about an aesthetic, it doesn't exist. What do you think about this? Can an aesthetic exist without someone talking about it?

—Michael Owen Jones, "The Concept of 'Aesthetic' in the Traditional Arts," *Western Folklore* 30 (1971): 77–104.

Ask students the following questions:

- If you were going to create a museum in your community based on the sport, what would you collect?
- How should the building look, and where would you want it to be?
- How would you display the items?
- Who would come to the museum? Would you call it an art museum? Why or why not?

Teachers and students can learn a lot about their community's aesthetics based on the activities community members are involved in during their leisure time. These leisure activities say a great deal about what individuals find pleasing. These activities are often based on what the local environment can provide, such as snow for snowboarding, or sand for making sandcastles. We even develop environments around these choices such as ski lodges and beach houses. One's choice of clothing and the design and purchase of a variety of objects used in sporting activities also becomes a factor. Art projects focusing on these ubiquitous and important parts of our lives demonstrate to students how the act of enjoying one activity can affect many other aesthetic choices and ways of living in a community.

Notes

1 For a discussion on reversals in lowriding cultural aes-
thetics, see Tomas Ybarra-Frausto, "Rasquachismo: A
Chicano Sensibility," in Richard Griswold del Castillo,
Teresa McKenna, and Yvonne Yarbro-Bejarano, eds.
Chicano Art: Resistance and Affirmation, 1965–1985 (Los
Angeles: Wight Art Gallery, UCLA, 1991), 155–62. A
more complete description of lowriding traditions, with
lots of information from the lowriders themselves, can
be found in Denise Sandoval and Patrick A. Polk, *Arte y
Estilo: The Lowriding Tradition* (Los Angeles: Petersen
Automotive Museum, 2000).

2 For a brief discussion on African-American yard art see
Lucy Lippard, *The Lure of the Local: Senses of Place in a
Multicentered Society* (New York: The New Press, 1997),
259.

3 For more information on the Kwanzaa project, see
Jacqueline Chanda and Vesta Daniel, "The Essences of
Contextual Understanding," *Art Education* 53, no. 2
(March 2000): 6–11.

4 For more information on this exhibition, see: Doug
Blandy and Kristin G. Congdon, "An Interdisciplinary
Response to a Folk Art Exhibit in a University Fine Art
Setting, "*Journal of Multi-cultural and Cross-cultural
Research in Art Education* 7, no. 1 (1989): 69–81; Doug
Blandy and Kristin G. Congdon, "Community Based
Aesthetics as an Exhibition Catalyst and a Foundation
for Community Involvement," *Studies in Art Education
29,* no. 4 (1998): 243–49; and Doug Blandy, Kristin G.
Congdon, and Michael Magada, "An Art Education
Response to a Folk Art Exhibition, *Viewpoints: Dialogues
in Art Education* (Spring 1987): 14–18.

5 Manuel Vega was a featured artist in the 1998 exhibition titled "Florida Folklife: Traditional Arts in
Contemporary Communities," organized by the
Historical Museum of Southern Florida in Miami. The
information here came from Bob Stone's article
"Manuel Vega," on page 68 in the catalog of the same
name, edited by Stephen Stuempfle.

6 The information presented here comes from two
sources: *Suzanne Lacy's Mapping the Terrain: New Genre
Public Art* (Seattle: Bay Press, 1995), 194–95, and a personal interview with Rigoberto Torres at his home in
Kissimmee, Florida, on October 8, 2000.

7 Information on the history of surfing can be found in
Drew Kampion's book, *Stoked: A History of Surf Culture*
(Santa Monica: General Publishing Group, 1997). The
quote and information on collecting surfing memora-
bilia came from Larry Bleibeg's article, "A Salute to
Those Who Blazed the Waves," in the *Orlando Sentinel*,
July 12, 1998, Sec. L, p.3.

Chapter

8

Art Programs Focusing
on Ethnicity

We all belong to an ethnic group—most likely more than one. We also hear more and more about how diverse the United States is and how it is increasingly becoming more multicultural. Community arts activists Don Adams and Arlene Goldbard claim that "the most obvious manifestation of our heterogeneity is ethnic diversity." They further profess that the art world has made attempts to create uniformity by delivering culture in a manner that disregards or devalues the artistic expressions of people of color.[1] By giving greater visibility and voice to more ethnic groups, we can work to eliminate the idea that valuable art is created by people from only a few ethnic groups.

This chapter will explore ethnicity as it relates to artistic products and processes. The emphasis here will be on ways to value our diverse ethnic backgrounds, while discovering new and perhaps more inclusive and positive ways of understanding and building on our artistic heritage. In order to be diverse in our study of art, we must explore artistic expressions that happen in various places in our communities, and not just in galleries and art museums. Because immigrants often settle in places where family and people from their home countries already live, arts rooted in ethnic traditions often thrive in certain regions. Indigenous peoples continue to create artistic works related to their heritages in their homelands. For example, Eskimos and Intuits continue to make fancy parkas, canoes, and kayaks; mountain dulcimers are often made by those whose ancestors came from Ireland; and windmills are common lawn ornaments in Dutch communities, especially in northeastern Iowa.[2]

Sometimes these artistic traditions thrive within communities, and sometimes they survive because of efforts from organizations outside the community. For example, the hula has survived, in large part, because it has been recreated for tourists in major Hawaiian hotels.[3] The experiences of many traditions rooted in ethnicity are enhanced when they are viewed in their original contexts. Lowriding traditions, for instance, are best seen on the street and not in a museum, and Mexican Day of the Dead *ofrendas*, or altars for the dead, are more powerful when they are created in the home for relatives, than in a museum for strangers to visit.

The term "ethnicity" is used as a cultural term to explore expressions ordinarily based on an individual's place of origin, or the place of origin of one's ancestors. A person need not have been born in Ireland for their Irish-American parents to have

instilled in them an appreciation for certain Irish traditions like shepherd's pie, Irish whiskey, four-leaf clovers, leprechauns, and the color green. Another example could be the use of Chinese chops (stamp or seal), which were traditionally used for business transactions like signatures. Since the art of making chops has been practiced in China for more than a thousand years, having a personal chop is still highly valued in many Chinese-American communities.

While it may seem that focusing on ethnicity in the classroom may separate us by explaining our differences, this focus is not intended to disregard the many things we have in common. What it does do is help us understand our diverse traditional experiences. It also gives us the opportunity to adapt some

8.1 Ofrenda, *by Catalina Delgado Truck. City Hall, Orlando, Florida, 1996. Photo by Kristin G. Congdon.*

of these experiences to fit our own circumstances. For example, if we are not Mexican but enjoy the idea of the Day of the Dead, we might better be able to relate to the altar-making experience by bringing it to our own culture. From there we can build on what we know, perhaps by adding a photograph, a glass of water, or a certain kind of flower to our own altar spaces. Learning about other traditional experiences helps us appreciate and expand on our own.

In focusing on ethnicity this chapter deliberately avoids a focus on race. Race is a cultural construct rather than a scientific one. In other words, race is a categorization used primarily for negative outcomes. Race has been used to suggest that there are natural differences among us, whereas, biologically speaking, racial categories are unsupportable, or at best problematic.[4] The roots of racial constructs come from the transatlantic slave trade and the establishment of economic systems that placed Africans at the bottom rung. Likewise, race was used to justify the extermination of millions of indigenous Americans. Categorization by race has been pervasive for several centuries in the United States, whereas ethnicity is a relatively new concept that comes from the social sciences and was invented to explain immigration patterns.[5]

A major point of this chapter is to recognize that many of the same things we do, we may do differently because of our ethnicity. For example, when we talk about "commuting to work," we should understand that this does not mean driving a car someplace for everyone. Many Hopi farmers, for example, whose farmlands surround their villages within a five- to ten-mile radius, commute to work (their fields) in the traditional manner, by running.[6] Both the Hopi farmer and the Jewish businesswoman in Chicago who gets in her car to go to

Try This

Research the Chinese idea of *feng shui*. Read the following quote:

"The general *feng shui* idea is that if a setting doesn't make you feel welcome, tinker with it until it does."

Identify a space where you spend a lot of time. Make a drawing of changes you would like to make to provide you with a more comfortable feeling in the space. After the drawing has been finished, invite a *feng shui* expert to look at the drawing to determine how it would fit into the Chinese approach to space.

—From Winifred Gallagher, *The Power of Place: How Our Surroundings Shape Our Thoughts, Emotions, and Actions* (New York: Poseidon Press, 1993), 143.

Try This

In the March/April 1993 issue of *Update (ArtTable)*, the American Council for the Arts had an article titled "Race, Ethnicity and Culture in the Visual Arts" (pp. 1-11). In it Kinshasha Holman Conwill said, "All museums are ethnically specific, whether it's the Whitney, the Met, El Museo or the Studio Museum. . . ."

Make a list of all the museums you can think of in your area. Beside each one, see if you can name its ethnic identification.

What's White, Anyway?

"In Argentina, where he was born, my acquaintance had always been on solid taxonomic ground. His race was no more a mystery than the color of the clouds. It was a fact, presumably rooted in biology, that he was as white as a man could be. But his move to the United States had left him confused. So he turned to me and sheepishly asked in Spanish, 'Am I white or am I Latino?'"

—From Ellis Cose, "What's White, Anyway?" *Newsweek* (September 18, 2000): 64.

work are acting in ethnic and environmental ways. This is not to say that the Hopi could not drive to work and the Jewish woman couldn't run; it only means that they are acting in traditional ways based on their traditional experiences. This chapter addresses our traditions (some of which may not be positive) and the dynamic ability people have to change and redefine traditional ethnic practices.

As was true in the previous chapters, not all the model programs and projects described here are centered on folklore. However, they all have folkloric aspects, finding their origins rooted in the community practices of ethnic groups.

"Yeast of Eden" at the Ziff Museum

In 1999, Miami's Ziff Museum had an exhibition called, "Yeast of Eden: Ethnic Breads in Florida," based on the awareness that so many Floridians come from somewhere else, or at least their parents or grandparents do. Curator Remko Jansonius worked with Jerry Beck from the Revolving Museum in Boston to present an exhibition based on this diversity. The result was a house made of bread. Like people, bread comes in many varieties. Out of a flavorful assortment of bread, a house was constructed, collectively and collaboratively made of intersecting textures, shapes, and traditions. Participants included artists, educators, businesspeople, and more than 450 students from 15 schools. The curator explained:

Students have collected family bread recipes; while exploring the origins of the recipes, they explored their families' origins and histories. They created artwork with bread and the kitchen as themes; thus they explored family dynamics and the roles that family members play in the preparation of food. They wrote stories and poetry based on bread. And finally, they have created "bread art," by painting and decorating pitas, matzot, bagels, Cuban breads, hotdog buns, tortillas, rye bread, and fry bread.[7]

The house of bread was a twelve-by-sixteen-by-fourteen-foot structure made entirely of ethnic breads. This exhibition reminds us that most all cultures eat bread, and that the kinds of breads they eat are often based in their ethnic identities. What is wonderful about this concept is that it celebrates diversity, while, at the same time, it points to what we all have in common. In this case, it is the making and eating of bread.

Classroom Connections: The Cultural Context of Bread

Teachers might see how many different kinds of breads their students can name. Students might be instructed to ask their parents and grandparents if their families have any traditional bread recipes, or if they remember the kinds of breads they ate when they were children. Add these bread names to the list. Students who come back without any information might be asked what kind of bread they usually eat at home. What kinds of breads has each student eaten? How would they describe the experience of

Quotes from Youth Participants in "Yeast of Eden"

"When my grandmother was young she was very poor. On Easter morning, she would run down from her bedroom and find some Italian Easter bread with very colorful eggs inside. She did not get anything else but she was very happy. She had many brothers and sisters who each got bread too. Our family has passed on the tradition of Easter bread for many generations."

—From Nicole Scotto, North Beach Elementary, Miami Beach

"My mother (Maria Alexander) used to tell me about tea-time in Sri-Lanka. Her mother always used to make special breads and cakes and the kitchen would fill with different aromas of baking, my mother recalled with fond memory. One of the items she used to make was Sultana Bread or Buns. This was one of my mother's and my grandmother's favorites. My great-grandmother used to add nuts and other dried fruits to make this recipe more special!

"Tea-time was a time for gathering of all the women in my mother's family for a little bit of afternoon chit-chat and family gossip. My mom recalls these good times with fond memory, since she used to get time to spend with her grandmother and all her aunts. Tea was either taken in the large family kitchen or on the outside veranda (patio), where there was plenty of shade from the hot tropical afternoon."

—From Eric Alexander, V.A.B. Highland Oaks Elementary, Miami

8.2 "Yeast of Eden: Ethnic Breads in Florida," 1999. Produced by the Sanford L. Ziff Jewish Museum of Florida, Miami Beach, in collaboration with Jerry Beck, Artistic Director, The Revolving Museum. Photo courtesy of the Jewish Museum.

The Bread That Means the Most

"The bread that means to me the most is a Cuban bread. Why it means to me the most is because I love it with butter; but it is good without it too. I can eat it any way, because it is my favorite. That is the bread that means to me the most."

—From Jessica Delgado, North Beach Elementary, Miami Beach

eating each kind of bread? Teachers can also ask students if they have made bread before and what that experience was like. Discuss special occasions or holidays where the breads are baked and eaten, along with the ethnic origin of each type of bread. Teachers, along with students and parents, can learn about the meanings these breads take on when baked and served in their ethnic context. Question students about what happens when the bread is removed from its context, and in what ways its meaning is different.

Students might be asked to explore the shape of their bread, and to design a house made of their traditional bread on paper. The class might study the various shapes of their breads and design another house composed of the variety of bread shapes.

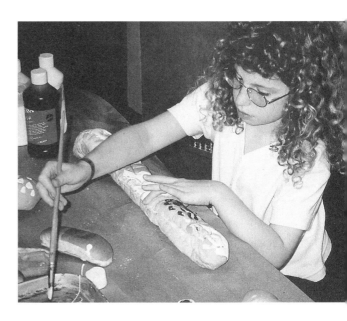

8.3 Miriam Kolker, third grader from North Beach Elementary School in Miami Beach, paints bread for "Yeast of Eden," 1999. Produced by the Sanford L. Ziff Jewish Museum of Florida, Miami Beach, in collaboration with Jerry Beck, Artistic Director, The Revolving Museum. Photo courtesy of the Jewish Museum.

Students might then write a paper describing which bread house from the class they like best and why. If the situation allows, an actual bread house could be designed and constructed, as was done at the Ziff Museum.

If this project is taken on, various questions about architectural style, engineering stability, and the function of the space need to be discussed. You could expand on this project by seeing what other kinds of foods, desserts for example, might have ethnic roots and then use them in a group project. Instead of a building, students can create a timeline based on what kinds of foods are eaten during particular times of the year. They can further describe, visually and in writing, what purpose the foods serve in each ritual or holiday celebration. The timeline can be placed in a hallway and it can serve as the structure for projects in both social studies and art. From each ethnic celebration and corresponding culinary traditions, lessons could be created revolving around costume, home decorations, dance, and music. In this way children can become cultural historians and share their family traditions with classmates.

Nevada's Shoshone Basketry and the Folk Arts Apprenticeship Program

Many states have Folk Arts Apprenticeship Programs.[8] Accomplished traditional artists are selected to teach someone from the same cultural group (often an ethnic group) a designated tradition. The tradition can be musical, narrative, or visual. From 1993 to 1995, Nevada gave apprenticeship awards to two groups of Shoshone basketry artists.

As a recognized expert in Shoshone basketry traditions, Evelyn Pete teaches the art to her sister, Edna Mike, who never learned to gather the willows and weave the traditional baskets. Willows are found at their home reservation, Blackeye Ranch, where they

Discussion Point

You have all heard the saying, "You are what you eat." Is it possible that we also become what we do? Read the following quote and discuss this question in light of various kinds of artists. The excerpt is from a novel; the author is speaking about Cash, a Cherokee Indian.

"But since he started putting beads on a needle each night, his eye never stops counting rows: pine trees on the mountainsides, boards in a fence, kernels on the ear of corn as he drops it into the kettle. He can't stop the habit, it satisfies the ache in the back of his brain, as if it might fill in his life's terrible gaps. His mind is lining up, making jewelry for someone the size of God."

—From Barbara Kingsolver, *Pigs in Heaven* (New York: HarperPerennial, 1993), 110.

were both born. In another apprenticeship, Lilly Sanchez, Edna and Evelyn's older sister, taught her daughter, Virginia Sanchez, to weave traditional baskets. Virginia explained the importance of learning family ethnic traditions, "It's kind of a responsibility, I think, that we all have. Especially when you have children, the responsibility then is to pass it on to them. For me to be able to learn this well and then teach her [Virginia's daughter] is real important to me."[9]

This example helps point out how many traditional arts are learned through the apprenticeship model. While we tend to think that information in the school curriculum centers on the most important kinds of knowledge, it is clear that much of the learning that takes place in community settings can also be powerfully relevant and enriching.

Classroom Connections: Artists Expanding on Classroom Curriculum

Teachers can contact their state's Arts Council or Division of Historical Resources to inquire if their state has ever had a Folk Arts Apprenticeship Program. If they have, ask them to send information on the artists who have been involved. If any of these artists live in the school's community, invite them to visit with the class to explain their art form.

Teachers can solicit help from their students in identifying traditional artists who might qualify for a Folk Arts Apprenticeship Award. Work together with your students to find out how to apply and encourage the artists to participate.

Students can be asked to explore their family's traditions to see if there are any artistic practices that the class could study. Explore the possibility that one of your students might have a knowledgeable relative that could teach the class about a particular ethnic tradition. Ask students to describe a time

when a parent, grandparent, or other family or community member taught them how to make something. While it may be difficult, it is important to explain that some traditions that are passed on from generation to generation are not appropriate to carry on. This message is best presented by members of the community who can talk about a tradition they learned from their ancestors that they now understand to be irrelevant or offensive. These traditions might have to do with slavery, war, or racism. This presentation will teach children that we can all make changes for the better, and that all human beings have both positive and negative aspects to their character.

Eileen Brautman's Ketubot

Eileen Brautman is an art teacher in the Miami-Dade County, Florida, schools. She is also a ketubah artist.[10] A ketubah is a wedding contract that contains a promise made by the groom to the bride. Brautman explained, "In it he promises to treat his bride in a manner befitting a Jewish husband and according to the laws of Moses. The tradition of illuminating the ketubah developed over time in parts of the world where it was considered worthy."[11] Brautman writes the promise in Hebrew in carefully penned calligraphy. On the borders she does cutwork of symbols selected by the couple. The outside images can be religious or personal. Finished ketubot are framed and usually placed in the bedroom or in a nearby hallway.

Brautman understands that only Jewish people can make a ketubah, since it is intricately connected to Jewish law and Jewish practices. However, she carefully translates the idea of the ketubah to the predominately Haitian and Hispanic students she teaches. She shares with them a ketubah she is creating, discusses its historical roots, and explains that it is based on a promise. A discussion on promises takes place and students are asked to write a promise they would like to make and illuminate. Work on their promise statements includes the study of calligraphy, the design and usage of a template (understanding positive and negative shapes), and the cutting out of the design. Some students use color in their works. Brautman observes that students have an interest in learning about art from another culture and that they like having "an opportunity to discuss similarities and differences."[12]

Classroom Connections: Translating and Engaging in Ethnic Traditions

Teachers might have their students engage in the activity described above after having someone knowledgeable talk about ketubah. Students would learn about the ketubah, discuss the idea of a promise, and like Eileen Brautman's students, create promise statements that are illuminated using calligraphy and design work. The final promise statement could be presented to someone related to the promise.

8.4 Eileen Brautman creating a ketubah. Photo by Bud Lee.

Discussion Point

Define what the word "appropriation" means in relation to the art world. Read the following quote and discuss when and if it is acceptable to appropriate images, forms, and artistic processes from a culture which is not your own. Does Lowery Sims have a point about how we appreciate art created by non-White people?

"[A]re artists who are really grappling with the challenge of creating visual statements that reflect a connection with their cultural heritage being recognized as they should be? Or is recognition reserved for those clever enough to work the scam well through appropriation from other cultures? Are we seeing a repeat of the story of Little Richard and Elvis Presley? Should it bother us that the Rolling Stones can do the 'Harlem Shuffle' but the Harlemites end up being the background singers?

"Yes, I think it should. In this country, it seems, we can appreciate the diluted adaptation more readily than we can the intense and vigorous original. . . . [B]lack, Hispanic, Native American or Asian American artists . . . have had an undeniable influence on the flavor of American culture as a whole—witness the popularity of reggae music, braided hair, kung fu, salsa, etc. But as in the past, the products of these cultures tend to be appreciated while their originators remain excluded from, or oppressed and exploited in, the arena of world and art politics."

—From Lowery S. Sims, "Race, Representation, and Appropriation," in *Race and Representation: Art/Film/Video*, Project Co-Directors, Maurice Berger and Johnnetta Cole (New York: Hunter College, 1987), 17–20.

Teachers might discuss the kinds of artistic expressions that it is improper to participate in if you are not a member of the ethnic group from which the tradition originated. For example, if students are not Northwest Coast Indians, should they be making totem poles in the Northwest Coast style? If students are not Hopi, should they make kachina dolls? As a class, explore when it is appropriate to make a ritualistic work of art but not use it in a traditionally ritualistic manner. Explain how meanings are changed when the makers of objects change. Using the example that Eileen Brautman presented, lead students in a discussion about other ways they might appropriately study certain religious works made by various ethnic groups.

8.5 Ketubah by Eileen Brautman. Photo courtesy of the Florida Folklife Programs, Division of Historical Resources. Created by Eileen Brautman.

8.6 Eileen Brautman (middle) with Samantha and Robert Rothbaum holding their ketubah, 1999. Photo courtesy of Samantha and Robert Rothbaum.

Fraktur birth and wedding documents are a Pennsylvania German tradition involving calligraphy and decorative motif and are another example of artistic traditions made by particular ethnic groups.

Students might take the idea presented in this tradition or that of the ketubah and make their own commemorative document related to something they choose to celebrate in a new way. After the document is completed, students can explain how they think the document should be used, who should keep it, and where it should be placed.

The following questions could be used to facilitate a discussion related to ethnicity:

• Do you become part of an ethnic cultural group by birth or gradually by participating in that culture?
• Is it possible to be born into an ethnic group and not really be part of it? How could that happen?
• Can you give an example of some ethnic cultural tradition that you have adapted that did not belong to you by birth? How did you adapt it? Did you do it respectfully? Explain your answer.

Monterey Peninsula Museum of Art's Museum on Wheels

Many museums have curricular packages that can help the art educator plan lessons on artistic traditions from various ethnic groups. The Monterey Peninsula's Museum on Wheels (MOW) is one model program that functions to "educate and enrich the diverse California community." Its goal is to provoke debate and the discussion of ideas through exhibitions and programs. The museum on wheels is a mobile museum, which brings "a collection of international, folk, ethnic, and tribal arts to schools in Monterey and neighboring counties."[13]

Most of the work in MOW is folk art from different cultures. Programs presented to schools focus on Africa, North America, Latin America, and Asia. Each presentation includes a slide show, music, dance, folk art demonstrations, and actual artifacts from the focus area. After an introductory assembly, the artifacts are displayed in a secure space, usually the library. Booklets on each area include maps, introductory essays, hands-on lesson plans, vocabulary, and a bibliography. The museum program helps the entire school build integrated curricula around a particular country and their artistic expressions.[14]

Classroom Connections: Designing a Museum on Wheels

Students might pretend to be the director of their own Museum on Wheels. The board of directors has determined that the mission of the museum is to represent the community. Teachers can help facilitate the development of students' museums by asking the following questions:

• What members of your community would you be most interested in serving? Why?
• Which ethnic groups would you want your museum to focus on and why?
• What kinds of art would you want to put in your museum and why?

Teachers might ask students to develop an outline for a booklet they can give out to visitors at their museum stops in various neighborhoods. Students can be instructed to research an example of art programming possibilities and deliver it to an art center or community group in the neighborhood.

Students can explore how they could create their own MOW for their school and community. Exploring such a project teaches students about the many aspects of organizational planning involved in this kind of endeavor.

Models for art programming and suggested classroom activities in this chapter help students recognize that ethnicity can strongly influence the art people make and enjoy. It can also influence the ways administrators think about creating museums and developing educational plans.

There are numerous cultural perspectives that can be studied and developed when a teacher takes a community-based approach to art programming and curriculum development. This book explores a few of the most apparent ways we culturally organize ourselves as human beings. Teachers can work with students to elaborate on ideas expressed in this book as they create new ways of basing their art practices on their own communities' culture.

Notes

1   Don Adams and Arlene Goldbard, *Crossroads: Reflections on the Politics of Culture* (Talmage, CA: DNA Press, 1990), 16.

2   For more information on windmill yard art in Iowa, see Steve Torrence Ohrn, ed., *Passing Time and Traditions: Contemporary Iowa Folk Artists* (Des Moines: Iowa State University Press, 1984), 89.

3   See Jerry Mander, *In the Absence of the Sacred: The Failure of Technology and the Survival of the Indian Nations* (San Francisco: Sierra Club Books, 1991), 334. The author observes how hula has changed because of the context. While it used to be an expression of Hawaiian religion, it now exists more as entertainment. In this case, cultural tourism has been a mixed blessing. It helped save an art form, while changing its function.

4   See Lucy Lippard's discussion of race on page 5 of her book *Mixed Blessings: New Art in a Multicultural America* (New York: Pantheon Books, 1990). Here, she follows the lead of Henry Louis Gates, Jr., who puts the term "race" in quotes. Jane Kramer, in her chapter "Letter from Europe" in *The Graywolf Annual Ten: Changing Community*, ed. Scott Walker (St. Paul: Graywolf Press, 1993), 57–100, explained, "There used to be one category for all immigrants in England who were not European and that was 'black.'" She further explains that to the English, "everybody who was not English was the same black stranger" (p. 97). The census categories changed in 1989.

5   See the article, "We Need New and Critical Study of Race and Ethnicity" by Manning Marable in *The Chronicle of Higher Education* 46, no. 25 (February 25, 2000): B4–B7 for a more complete discussion of how problematic the terms "race" and "ethnicity" are. Marable explores new scholarship done in this area, and asks for more clarity and debate on the topic.

6   Mander, *In the Absence of the Sacred,* 269.

7   Quotation from the essay by Remko Jansonius "Yeast of Eden: Ethnic Breads in Florida" in the catalog, Remko Jansonius, *Yeast of Eden: Ethnic Breads in Florida* (Miami: Sanford L. Ziff Jewish Museum of Florida in collaboration with the Revolving Museum, 1999), 6–7. This catalog contains poetry and drawings by students as well as bread recipes.

8   Often these programs are funded by the National Endowment for the Arts, but sometimes states find other funding sources.

9   Information for this section came from the booklet titled *Nevada Folk Arts Apprenticeship 1993–1995* (Carson City, NV: Nevada State Council on the Arts, 1995), 10, 22.

10   "Ketubah" is the singular form of this Hebrew word, and "Ketubot" is the plural form.

11   Eileen Glickman Brautman, "Artist Statement," given to the author in 1999.

12   One art educator, when hearing about this lesson, said he would feel uncomfortable if a teacher asked his son or daughter to make a promise in school. An art teacher might want to select another word such as "contract" or "goal."

13   Information in this paragraph comes from the program brochure.

14   For more information on the Monterey Peninsula Museum of Art's Museum on Wheels, see Sandra Still's article, "Monterey Museum of Art Outreach Programs Add Much to Art Education," *Arts and Activities* (September 1997): 37–39 and "Museum Reaches Out to Migrant Students" also by Sandra Still in *Arts and Activities* (June 1999): 22–23 and 65. The museum address is: 559 Pacific Street, Monterey, CA 93940.

Acknowledgments

I would like to thank so many people for helping with this book. First, my thanks goes to Marilyn Stewart, who believed in this project and offered helpful suggestions throughout the process. I extend my sincere thanks to Wyatt Wade, David Coen, Georgiana Rock, and Jeannet Leendertse, who skillfully coordinated the publication process. I thank my longtime friend Doug Blandy, whom I credit with many of the ideas and projects highlighted in these pages. I am grateful for the continual assistance I have received from Tina Bucuvalas, Florida's State Folklorist, who knows far more about folklore than I do. My sincere appreciation goes to artists and educators Eileen Brautman and Karen Branen, who tried out projects in the classroom. Thanks to Remko Jansonius, who helped construct the Bread House in "Yeast of Eden" and drew my attention to it. Appreciation also goes to those who allowed me to use their photographs: The Florida Folklife Programs, Division of Historical Resources, Florida's Department of State, The Randall V. Mills Archives at the University of Oregon, Crealde School of Art in Winter Park, and to photographers Bud Lee and Peter Schreyer. Without information from Rick Lowe, Sandra Still, Gregory Hansen, Paddy Bowman, Laurie Hicks, and many, many others, this book would have been so much less than it is. And to Michael Owen Jones, who inspired me over twenty years ago, I continue to salute you with great admiration.

Kristin G. Congdon

Appendix

The following suggestions for community-based art activities are offered as ideas that the educator can adapt and develop. Many activities come from communities where the projects have actually taken place.

Suppose a tour bus is coming to your community for a visit. You are in charge of cultural tourism and must direct the group to the best sites. Create a visual map of places you think they would be interested in seeing.

In Kenya, detailed maps of rainfall are made with seeds placed on the ground. After a drawing of the landscape is scratched into the earth, colorful seeds are used to highlight certain areas. Looking at the many ways maps have been made, and thinking about the ways they could be made, some artists are imagining approaches to map-making that include being stitched and woven, danced, sung, or told in stories. Take a traditional map of a place that interests you and remake it in an unusual way.[1]

Visit a community where poverty is widespread. Talk to community members about what they see as positive about their neighborhood. Design a T-shirt reflecting the positive aspects of the community.

Holiday celebrations often extend beyond what is traditional. For example, many people place Christmas wreaths on their cars, and sometimes trees are placed on cranes on construction sites. Another old construction tradition is to place a lighted Christmas tree on top of buildings under construction. During a holiday season, take pictures of unusual holiday traditions in your community. See if you can discover the roots of the traditions.

Visit a family member or neighbor who has lived in your community for a long time. Ask to look at old photographs of local places. Go to the same places and take photographs of how they look today. Discuss what changes have been made. Draw pictures of how you would like the same spaces to look in twenty-five years. Do an exhibit of your work and invite local people to come and comment on the past, present, and future.

Many African-American women, especially in the South, wear elaborate hats to church. Find a church where these hats are worn and visit it on a Sunday. See if you can find out who makes the hats and why so many church members wear them.

Visit a restaurant that is a hang-out for local residents. Describe what kind of artwork you would suggest for the space. Explain why you chose it. Was your intention to reinforce the community aesthetic or expand it?

Read the children's book *Family Pictures: Cuadros de Familia* (San Francisco; Children's Book Press, 1990) by Mexican-American artist Carmen Lomas Garza. Discuss the family traditions depicted in the pictures and describe similar traditions you have in your family. Draw pictures of these traditions.

Look into issues that seem to divide members of your community. They might be related to economic inequality, immigration, homosexuality, employment, education, or housing. Study the issue and make a poster or banner that will help unite your community around the issue.

The following phrases are titles for workshops offered at The Findhorn Foundation in Scotland. Imagine you are an art educator hired to teach there. Write a description for each event.
Permaculture[2] Design Course
Deep Time and the Ecological Self
Finding the Inspiration Within

Create a pathway of cement stepping-stones in a public space. Each stone should have the footprint (real or invented) of a local hero/heroine. Each stone should, in some way, reflect the life of the honored person.

Go to your local shopping mall. View it, or a portion of it, as if it were an art museum. Write an art critique about the "exhibition." Evaluate the experience. What did you learn?

1   In Lucy Lippard's book, *The Lure of the Local: Senses of Place in a Multicentered Society* (New York: The New Press, 1997), 76, she talks about Doug Aberley's idea on how local empowerment can take place through home-made map making. These mappings would provide people with a creative outlet to describe what it is they actually know about the places in which they live.
2   The word "permaculture" means sustainable ecological living.

Fieldworker's Information Sheet
Artist Interview

Date: _____

Fieldworker: _____

Interviewed

Artist: _____

Address: _____

_____

_____

Place of Interview: _____

_____

_____

Place and Date of Birth: _____

_____

Ethnic Heritage: _____

Occupation: _____

Religion: _____

Family Members: _____

_____

_____

_____

Educational Background: _____

_____

_____

_____

Description of Artwork: _____

_____

_____

_____

Function/Use of Artwork: _____

_____

_____

_____

_____

Glossary

buckaroos Cowboys generally found in the Northwest part of the United States. They often have fancy saddles, belt-buckles, and other cowboy-related gear that communicates a pride in their traditions.

carnival A celebration related to Mardi Gras, only more associated with Caribbean culture than the Gulf Coast of the United States. It is a springtime ritual with parades, floats, costumes, and informal and formal parties that is associated with Easter. Carnival's roots are a synthesis of traditions from French/Spanish, Native American, and African/Afro-Caribbean performance styles.

chickees Seminole and Miccosukee architectural structures built from thatched palmetto fronds or cabbage leaves with cypress posts and rafters. Historically, separate chickees were built for cooking and sleeping. Two people working diligently can build them in a matter of two days. The basic shape is rectangular, although circular and square chickees can also be found. Chickees are still being built in Florida and can be seen as secondary structures to many of Florida's Native American homes.

crackers Self-sufficient individuals, often of Anglo or Celtic heritage, who settled in the rural southern states. Most often, they make their living from farming and raising live-stock. The 1976 election of Jimmy Carter to the presidency resulted in an interest in what has been called Cracker Chic.

community A group of people who share common beliefs, a way of life, place or neighborhood, occupation, recreation, or sense of purpose. Ordinarily, individuals in a community are drawn together through some kind of shared activity or interest.

comparsa Cuban dance with African roots performed in conga lines, often in the streets during public celebrations. The music is mostly made by drums, along with cowbells and skillets played with drumsticks. Fancy dresses of satin and organza are often worn by the female dancers. The word comparsa means "masquerade group" or "stage company."

Day of the Dead or *Días de los Muertos* A celebration, most often found in Mexico and the southwestern United States, in which deceased friends and relatives are said to come back to visit. Rituals generally take place on November 1st (All Saint's Day) and November 2nd (All Souls' Day). Families construct commemorative altars (*ofrendas*) and decorate graves with flowers and candles.

dogtrot house Vernacular architectural style of home where an open hallway separates two rooms under a gable roof. Typically built of logs, it was popular in the southeastern United States in the late eighteenth and early nineteenth centuries.

fichas Domino tiles used by Cubans and Cuban Americans.

folk beliefs Sometimes also referred to as superstitions by outsiders, they are generally associated with ideas held by the uneducated. However, a folklorist would says that all people, regardless of educational level have beliefs associated with their cultural groups.

folk groups Groups of people who hold shared beliefs and cultural practices. Folklorists generally use this term, whereas sociologists call these groups "subcultures." Inside group members generally understand the humor and gossip that is passed on by group members, while an outsider does not.

folk speech A way of talking that is peculiar to a specific folk group. It includes figures of speech, localized expressions, grammatical structures, and vernacular pronunciations.

folklife Often used interchangeably with folklore, it generally refers to the lived experience of folk groups.

folklore An area of study that has been referred to as "artistic communication in small groups" and "the aesthetics of everyday life." Among other things, folklore includes myths, legends, folktales, jokes, charms, blessings, riddles, curses, rituals, folk architecture, and material culture. The field of folklore focuses on creative cultural expressions that are often undervalued, especially in elite society.

folklorists Scholars who study traditional cultural groups along with their stories, material culture, and beliefs. They are interested not only in the product, but the creative processes involved in the making, appreciation, and transmission of the traditions.

herramientas Metal tools used in the worshipping rituals of individual deities of the Orisha or Santería religion. The Orisha community is strong in both Cuba and Miami. It maintains the religious traditions of the Yoruba people of contemporary Nigeria. *Herramientas* are used in both the consecration of an Orisha representation in a shrine, as well as those regalia used by the worshippers or the Orisha.

junkanoo Bahamian tradition, closely associated with Christmas season celebrations, with music and dance-like movements. Costumes for Junkanoo parades consist of hats, shirts, skirts, and pants primarily made of strips of crepe paper cut into fringe. In recent years, costumes are also adorned with felt, satin, beads, mylar, and colored plastic jewels.

ketubah A Jewish wedding contract, usually a promise the groom makes to a bride. While the word "ketubah" is Hebrew, the text is traditionally written in Aramaic, a language reflective of Hebrew. The contract is often decorated with meaningful symbols. The plural is ketubot.

Kwanzaa African-American holiday, created in 1966, it is celebrated from December 26 to January 1. Kwanzaa, meaning "first fruits of the harvest" in Swahili, is observed with the lighting of a candle for seven days. Each candle represents a focus on one of the cultural principals that African Americans should live by. They are: unity, self-determination, collective work and responsibility, cooperative economics, purpose, creativity, and faith. The candles are placed on an altar and decorated with fruits and vegetables. Small gifts (often handmade) are exchanged, African-based dishes are cooked and served to guests, and the ancestors are recognized and celebrated with music and dance.

lowriders Customized transportation made by Mexican Americans (sometimes called Chicanos). Typically a male-dominated activity, a lowrider can transform an automobile, van, or motorcycle's interior and/or exterior. Chrome is valued, as is a plush interior, a heavy-duty hydraulic system, a new and shiny paint job, and often a stylized mural. The vehicle is generally lowered to within a few inches of the road. The aesthetic is "low, slow, mean, and clean." Young boys, and sometimes girls, who are not of driving age customize bicycles.

Masons The oldest and largest fraternal society in the Western part of the world, originating primarily in Britain. Only a few aspects of the group are secret; these include certain salutations and dramatic rituals. Masonic lodges maintain homes for orphans and the elderly as well as specialized hospitals. Gravestones of deceased members of Masonic lodges often have Masonic symbols engraved on them.

material culture Tangible, humanmade objects and forms that represent cultural ideas and traditions. Material culture includes architecture, food, agriculture, medicine, home furnishings, dress, and art.

mehandi An East Indian practice of decorating the hands and feet with intricate designs. Practiced over a thousand years, the patterns are made with a mixture of henna and eucalyptus oil. Most commonly worn on joyous occasions like weddings, they symbolize good fortune and prosperity. Decorating a bride with elaborate designs could take two days, during which a number of rituals will take place, separating the bride from her family.

ofrendas Commemorative altars for the dead, most often constructed for the Day of the Dead (typically November 1st and 2nd) in Mexican and Mexican American cultures. They are filled with food, flowers, candles, photographs, and other items associated with the deceased.

ritual A custom often performed to affect the future, almost always to some practical end. To perform a ritual is to have a dialogue between order and disorder. Ritual action is often learned in youth, and instruction in it is often a part of initiation ceremonies. Rituals are often accompanied with costumes and accessories that are reserved for the specific event.

pakèts congo Magical charms associated with Haitian Voodoo. Priests and priestesses make them for clients as protection against negative forces. Created from cloth, they always have a round shape; inside the wrapped bundles are sweet-smelling herbs and medicinal leaves. The outside is decorated with lace, feathers, and sequins. The colors used have to do with the Iwa or spirit being represented. Songs and magical incantations take place as the pakét is made.

papel picado Cut paper work used on Mexican Day of the Dead ofrendas, but also used as decorative banners in both Mexico and other Latin American countries. In Mexico, they are traditionally made in pads of 25 or 50 sheets of tissue paper. A design is drawn on the top sheet and then cut using a small metal chisel and a hammer. The cheap, temporary tissue symbolizes the elusive nature of the mortal human. Common themes for papel picado are human and animal skeletons engaged in various day-to-day activities.

pysanky Ukrainian Easter eggs decorated by using a wax-resist technique and a series of dye baths. A Ukrainian myth explains that the Madonna brought eggs to Pontius Pilate, seeking to ask him to spare Christ's life. When her request was refused, she cried. Tears fell on the eggs and turned into brilliant colors. The eggs rolled to the ends of the earth and stopped where a dragon was held in chains. Each decorated egg is believed to add a link to the chain that keeps evil in check.

quinceañera Birthday parties for girls from Latin cultures turning fifteen. This is a celebration of her transition from childhood to womanhood. During this event, the girl wears an elaborate, floor-length white dress and dances a special waltz.

santero Spanish word for an artist who carves or paints saints or *santos.*

santos Holy personages, or saints, carved by Hispanic artists. While they are still created today, they were especially prolific from 1750–1850.

shotgun house Often associated with African-American neighborhoods, these homes are vernacular architecture in the South, characterized by their shape, which is generally one room wide and three rooms deep. It was said that you could shoot a bullet through the front door and it would exit out the back door without ever hitting any of the house's walls.

Index

About the Author

Kristin G. Congdon has taught art in a variety of settings and has published extensively on the study of folk arts, community arts, and contemporary art issues. She is coeditor, with Doug Blandy, of *Art in a Democracy* and *Pluralistic Approaches to Art Criticism;* with Doug Boughton, of *Evaluating Art Education Programs in Community Centers;* and, with Paul Bolin and Doug Blandy, of *Remembering Others: Making Invisible Histories of Art Education Visible* and *Histories of Community-Based Art Education.* Additionally, Congdon is the author of *Uncle Monday and Other Florida Tales* and coauthor, with Kara Kelley Hallmark, of *Artists from Latin American Cultures.* She is currently professor of film and philosophy at the University of Central Florida.